BUYER BEWARE

BUYER BEWARE

Finding Truth in the Marketplace of Ideas

Janet Parshall

MOODY PUBLISHERS

CHICAGO

Scripture quotations marked NIV are taken from the *Holy Bible, New International Version*®, NIV®. Copyright © 1973, 1978, 1984 by Biblica, Inc.™ Used by permission of Zondervan. All rights reserved worldwide.

Scripture quotations marked KJV are taken from the King James Version.

Scripture quotations marked ESV are taken from *The Holy Bible, English Standard Version*. Copyright © 2000, 2001 by Crossway Bibles, a division of Good News Publishers. Used by permission. All rights reserved.

Scripture quotations marked NASB are taken from the *New American Standard Bible*®, Copyright © 1960, 1962, 1963, 1968, 1971, 1972, 1973, 1975, 1977, 1995 by The Lockman Foundation. Used by permission. (www.Lockman.org)

Scripture quotations marked NKJV are taken from the *New King James Version*. Copyright © 1982 by Thomas Nelson, Inc. Used by permission. All rights reserved.

Scripture quotations marked NLT are taken from the *Holy Bible, New Living Translation*, copyright © 1996, 2004. Used by permission of Tyndale House Publishers, Inc., Wheaton, Illinois 60189, U.S.A. All rights reserved.

Edited by Annette LaPlaca
Interior design: Ragont Design
Cover design: Smartt Guys design
Cover image: Svitlana Pavzyuk/Bigstock
Author Photo: Courtesy of Moody Bible Institute

Library of Congress Cataloging-in-Publication Data

Parshall, Janet.
 Buyer beware : finding truth in the marketplace of ideas / Janet Parshall.
  p. cm.
 Includes bibliographical references.
 ISBN 978-0-8024-0561-6
 1. Christian life. 2. Christianity and culture. 3. Bible. O.T. Jeremiah--Criticism, interpretation, etc. I. Title.
 BV4501.3.P3735 2012
 261--dc23
                              2012023830

Moody Publishers is committed to caring wisely for God's creation and uses recycled paper whenever possible. The paper in this book consists of 10 percent post-consumer waste.

We hope you enjoy this book from Moody Publishers. Our goal is to provide high-quality, thought-provoking books and products that connect truth to your real needs and challenges. For more information on other books and products written and produced from a biblical perspective, go to www.moodypublishers.com or write to:

Moody Publishers
820 N. LaSalle Boulevard
Chicago, IL 60610

1 3 5 7 9 10 8 6 4 2

Printed in the United States of America

To my fellow pilgrims, past and present.
Like Bunyan's classic characters, you have courageously
entered Vanity Fair on your way home to the Celestial City.
Along the journey, you have loved His Word passionately
and longed to share it with a watching, seeking, hurting world.
I have learned so much from you as you've boldly
and bravely dared to look the merchants of Vanity Fair
in the face with your eyes of love and the heart of a lion,
declaring His Truth. The marketplace of ideas
has been changed forever because of you.

Contents

Just as Christian came up to the Cross,
his burden loosed from off his shoulders,
fell from off his back, and began to tumble
down the hill, and so it continued to do till it
came to the mouth of the sepulcher.
There it fell in, and I saw it no more!

John Bunyan, *The Pilgrim's Progress*

INTRODUCTION
A Profane Pilgrim

He was a profane man, by his own admission. His friends even commented at his particular prowess for cursing. He would say of himself that he was the "the ungodliest fellow for swearing they ever heard."[1] In short, he was, in his own words, "a very great, profane sinner, and an illiterate poor man."[2]

John Bunyan was a tinker, by trade. The rough country life of the Borough of Bedford, England, rarely afforded people the luxury of buying new pots, so mending old pots created an opportunity for John to eke out a meager living.

But Bunyan was a man with a disquieted spirit. He may have been able to repair pots, but he didn't know how to repair the hole in his heart. He struggled with his own sins, wondering if he had committed the "unpardonable sin" and if it might be too late for his soul.

It wasn't. Bunyan met John Gifford, a local pastor who had persecuted Puritans before he accepted Christ as his Savior. After hearing Gifford preach, John Bunyan found the grace of God to be truly amazing and came to the place where he readily received what God has done for each of us. He marveled that one so vile, a mere tinker from Bedford, could come to know the power of the Cross and the joy of forgiveness.

Scripture tells us, "For the mouth speaks what the heart is full of" (Matthew 12:34 NIV) and that certainly was the case with Bunyan. He spent hours studying Scripture, became active in Gifford's church, and felt a clear call on his life to proclaim the Truth that had so completely set him free. Bunyan was immersed so deeply in the Word of God that Charles Spurgeon once said of him, "Prick him anywhere; his blood is Bibline, the very essence of the Bible flows from him."[3]

In 1655, Bunyan began his preaching career. The same mouth that once hurled curses now proclaimed the unconditional love of the Savior. He wouldn't stop. He *couldn't* stop. Like Peter and John before him, he could not "help speaking about what [he had] seen and heard" (Acts 4:20 NIV). His sins had been forgiven, and that news was simply too good to keep to himself.

John Owen, a well-known preacher of that day, would often go to hear Bunyan preach. Bunyan was self-taught; Owen was a graduate of Oxford University. Yet something about the messages of Bunyan drew Owen, a famous and renowned preacher, to listen for hours to what the repairer of pots had to say. When asked by King Charles II why he would go and listen to an uneducated man, Owen responded, "May it please your Majesty, could I possess the tinker's ability for preaching, I would willingly relinquish all my learning."[4]

But there were those who felt Bunyan should be silenced. In 1658, he was indicted for preaching without a license—an effective charge for silencing someone with whom the ruling authorities of the day disagreed. Preachers of his day were required not only to register with the government but additionally to agree never to preach any doctrine at odds with the Church of England. Therein lay the problem.

John's message was simply the message of salvation by *faith* and *grace* alone. His message was deemed politically incorrect and did not reflect the majority opinion of the day. Bunyan was undeterred.

In 1660, in mid-sermon, two sheriffs from the king arrived with an arrest warrant and took John Bunyan off to jail. It would not be his last trip to the prison of Bedford.

Prisons of the 1600s bear no resemblance to the prisons of today. There were no clean cots, no workout rooms, no education programs, no television sets, and very little light. Bunyan found darkness, disease, and destitution. In those days, more people died in prison than were released from them. Bunyan's daily companions were the lice, the rats, and plenty of other prisoners. There was no privacy, no sanitation, and no hope. John Bunyan's first imprisonment lasted twelve years. There would be others.

Bunyan took with him to prison two invaluable tools—his knowledge of the world and his knowledge of the Word. Even in bondage, John knew that God was sovereign and had not abandoned him.

In response to a letter of encouragement he had received in prison, Bunyan penned a poem entitled *Prison Meditations* that reads, in part:

> I am indeed in prison now
> In body, but my mind
> Is free to study Christ, and how
> Unto me He is kind.
>
> For tho' men keep my outward man
> Within their locks and bars,
> Yet by the faith of Christ I can
> Mount higher than the stars.
>
> Their fetters cannot spirits tame,
> Nor tie up God from me;
> My faith and hope they cannot lame;
> Above them I shall be.[5]

As horrific as it was to be separated from his family and as physically isolating and mentally challenging as his imprisonment was, John Bunyan saw God at work. During his captivity, Bunyan sought the heart of his Savior—and found it.

While in jail, John devoured the Scriptures daily. He contemplated, hour by hour, the life of a Christian. What did it mean to be a follower of Jesus? Are there universal experiences that all believers have? Can

Christians expect certain challenges and battles in their walk with the Lord?

His rich imagination and his love of the Word inspired John Bunyan to pen the classic *Pilgrim's Progress*. Second only to the Bible, his book has been read by more people than any other book in English Literature.[6]

Bunyan used allegory to tell his tale. He wanted readers to see themselves in the adventures that Christian, the main character of the story, experienced. The doubts, struggles, sufferings, and victories of the Christian life took on an allegorical life of their own in *Pilgrim's Progress*.

So friend, let me stop here for a moment. You have waded in to this book thus far. I can assume that, at a minimum, you are curious as to where this book will take you. In truth, this book is more about following than leading.

If, like Bunyan of old, you and I are willing to follow Jesus whenever and wherever He will take us, then you and I should be prepared to go where we are sometimes not wanted. We should expect to be marginalized for our beliefs, and we should anticipate that being outside our "comfort zone" is very much going to be the standard if obedience is our goal.

Will it be easy? Ask John Bunyan. Sitting within the dank, rancid walls of the Bedford prison was no picnic. But out of the incubator of that experience was birthed a timeless classic that still compels us to follow Him—no matter what—*all* the way to the Celestial City.

You and I can travel together for a bit. We won't be alone, just like Bunyan was never alone. We will be accompanied by the One who will make the journey unforgettable and so very worthwhile.

If you are ready, let's go!

SECTION 1
Finding Our
Place in
the World

And diff'ring judgments serve but to declare
That truth lies somewhere, if we knew but where.

William Cowper, "Hope"

Buy the truth, and do not sell it;
Buy wisdom, instruction, and understanding.

Proverbs 23:23 ESV

1
The Marketplace

T hen I saw in my dream that they had left the wilderness and entered a town where there was a fair that continued all year long. . . . The name of the town was Vanity, and the fair was Vanity Fair. The people of the town were vain, caring for nothing but money, pleasure, and fame. The town was very old, and the fair had been going for many, many years.

Almost five thousand years ago, pilgrims, on their way to the Celestial City, went through this town. Finally, Beelzebub, Apollyon, and Legion, with their laborers, set up this fair to provide every kind of entertainment for travelers and to sell all types of merchandise all year long. And still, at this fair is sold such merchandise as fine houses, lands, stocks and bonds, false security, gay clothing, jewelry, expensive cosmetics, gold and silver, antiques, pearls, precious stones, fame, fortunes, reputations, virtue, honor, popularity, positions, phony titles, counterfeit degrees, contests, chances, games, votes, elections, government offices, personal influences, padded reports, propaganda, falsehoods, fictitious news, deceptions, artificial personalities, schemes, tricks, comics, beauty queens, sex appeal, prostitutes, human lives, and souls of men.

Moreover, at this fair at all times are gambling, juggling, cheating, defrauding, embezzling, lying, stealing, swindling, rogues, knaves, libertines, carnivals, festivities, drinking, revelries, conniving, fools, thugs, lewd women, murders, adulteries, and all kinds of immoralities. The broad road that leads to destruction which brings the fair much trade lies through the town.

And in this town of Vanity are taverns, night clubs, roadhouses, seductive shows, popular casinos, culture societies, fashionable churches, synthetic Christians, sectarian denominational segregation, professional pastors (using mass psychology, setting themselves up as lords over God's heritage, ruling their congregations for "filthy lucre," beating and fleecing their flocks instead of feeding them or setting them a good example). There are also famous pseudo scientists, charlatan physicians, clandestine bookmakers, racketeers—impostors of all kinds.

But, if anyone going to the Celestial City would miss this town of Vanity, he must of necessity go out of the world. The Prince of Peace, when here on earth, went through this town to His own country; and this same Beelzebub was then— as now—lord of the fair. He tried to sell the Prince many of his vanities. He even offered to make him manager of the fair. Because the Prince was such an influential person, Beelzebub led Him from section to section and showed Him all the various nations of the world and promised to make Him ruler over all, if He would but cheapen himself and buy some of his vanities. But the Prince did not care for any of the merchandise, and He left the town without spending a penny for any of Beelzebub's goods.

Now, as soon as Christian and Faithful entered the fair they created a sensation, not only in the fair but throughout the town.

First, their dress was so different from the people of the place that everyone gazed at them. Some said they were crank; some called them outlandish others said they were there to create trouble.

Second, their speech was different. Few could understand what they said, for naturally they spoke the language of Canaan, while those who kept the fair were men of this world. From one end of the fair to the other, they seemed like barbarians.

Third, these pilgrims showed no interest in their goods, and this worried the people of the fair most. Christian and Faithful did not even care to see them, and when they were asked to buy they would stop up their ears and say, "Turn away my eyes from beholding vanity," (Psalm 119:37 KJV) looking upward as if they belonged to another country.

One who had already heard of the men, observing their peculiar behavior,

16

mockingly said to them, "What will you buy?" Then they fastened their eyes upon him and said, "We buy the truth."[1]

Those words from the pen of John Bunyan were first published in 1678, but they are amazingly apropos for the twenty-first century. As this part of the adventure begins, Christian, the main character of *Pilgrim's Progress*, is found traveling with his friend, Faithful. Bunyan, using allegory, gave each of his characters specific names that exemplify certain attributes. This great teacher wanted each part of the journey to reveal some aspect of our travels with the Savior, this side of glory.

"Christian," for example, is the story's protagonist and represents each one of us after we come to faith in Jesus Christ. Early in the story, Christian was called "Graceless" as he did not yet know the amazing grace offered to all because of what was done on Calvary's cross.

But Graceless's name changes after he meets "Evangelist" (a perfect name for one who is willing to share the Truth of God's Word, or *evangelize*), who introduces him to "the book" (the Bible) and starts Graceless (now Christian) on the way to the Celestial City (heaven).

Evangelist and Christian soon part, and Christian is joined by a new companion, Faithful. But these two Pilgrims soon find that their path necessarily takes them right through a long-standing fair called "Vanity Fair." Bunyan chose to underscore the words of Ecclesiastes by pointing out the "vanity" of this world when he gave the fair its name. But Bunyan also wanted to convey something else: We Pilgrims can't get to the Celestial City (heaven) without going through Vanity Fair. It is part of the journey, and it is unavoidable. You and I, fellow Pilgrim, must also pass through this lusty "fair."

In truth, when John Bunyan wrote about Vanity Fair, he could have been writing about our culture today. He noted that people at "the fair" cared for nothing but fame, money, and pleasure. Harkening again to Ecclesiastes, Bunyan intimates that there is "nothing new under the sun" (Ecclesiastes 1:9 NIV) by noting that the fair has been around for a long time. Humankind has been chasing after these vanities, and many more like them, since time immemorial. Sadly, we recognize that there are those who are always readily available to "sell" shabby goods (bad ideas) and just as many "customers" willing to "buy" them.

Have you ever visited a real marketplace? My husband and I have been in many in various places around the world. I remember the first time we visited the Old City in Jerusalem. As we walked under the arches that covered the cobblestone streets from the time the Romans occupied that great city, we moved past burlap bags filled with colorful spices. The smell of fresh fish and newly baked bread punctuated the air. Shop after shop, stacked tightly next to each other, lined one narrow street after another. Baskets, jewelry, olive oil, leather goods, caftans—all kinds of trinkets hung from the doorways, giving the potential customer no shortage of opportunities to buy.

Merchants pushed their carts up and down the smooth stones, trod by so many for thousands of years. Shopkeepers would come out of their little stores and shout, "You want to buy? You *American*? I give you good price!"

The average tourist learns quickly that charlatans abound and the same kind of merchandise can cost one price at one shop and be markedly more or less expensive at another shop around the corner.

If you don't know where you are going or what you are looking for, you can quickly lose your way. It is very easy to feel overwhelmed and out of your comfort zone. Being a successful shopper in the Old City requires a certain amount of grit and boldness measured with just the right amount of American diplomacy. No tourist ever wants to represent the "ugly American." And no one can go to Jerusalem *without* visiting the marketplace. It is simply a part of the journey.

But just like any traveler can quickly lose their way in the Old City, the "vanities" Bunyan wrote about can take any Pilgrim off the straight and narrow path. The apostle John knew this when he wrote, "For all that is in the world, the lust of the flesh, and the lust of the eyes, and the pride of life, is not of the Father, but is of the world" (1 John 2:16 KJV).

The lust of the flesh, the lust of the eyes, and the pride of life—the prince of this world still uses the same tried and tested areas of enticement to get us off the path. There really is "nothing new under the sun."

Bunyan readily identified some of those lusts, recognizing that "No temptation has overtaken you that is not common to man" (1 Corinthians 10:13 ESV). While he was writing in the late 1600s, Bunyan could just as easily have been writing about the same sins that plague us in the twenty-first century—lying, drunkenness, gossiping, sexual immorality, and even murder, just to name a few.

Let's face it: Vanity Fair *was* and still *is* a rough place.

The reformed tinker knew that people would gravitate toward carnal pleasures; he pointed out hypocrisy in the Church and recognized that mandate for Christian character and how easily its absence could be detected.

Let's face it: Vanity Fair *was* and still *is* a rough place. Surely Christian and Faithful would have preferred the gentle countryside that lay not far from the fair. After all, who really wants to go into all that messy stuff—the shouting, the stealing, the lying, the sexual promiscuity, the turning of Truth on its head?

There was no delight for these two Pilgrims in being ridiculed by the merchants of Vanity Fair for the way they dressed. Even the way they spoke was mocked. Bunyan said they "spoke the language of Canaan" but the merchants were men of the world. Remember how Bunyan himself had struggled in this area? Profanity and vulgarity peppered the merchants' speech—but not Christian's and Faithful's.

Most infuriating of all to the street venders was the reality that the two Pilgrims showed no interest in the merchandise being sold at the fair. It didn't take long for the "sellers" to note that the Pilgrims were not "buyers." Christian and Faithful were mocked, derided, marginalized, and ridiculed.

Fellow Pilgrim, there is no way around it. Our Pilgrim's progress will necessarily take us right through Vanity Fair. In fact, that is exactly where we are told to go.

God was gracious in preserving His Word, a very personal conversation between the Father and His Son. In John 17, we quietly lean in to hear a passionate prayer of the Savior to His Father for His disciples. Jesus says:

> I am coming to you now, but I say these things while I am still in the world, so that they may have the full measure of my joy within them. I have given them your word and the world has hated them, for they are not of the world any more than I am of the world. *My prayer is not that you take them out of the world* but that you protect them from the evil one. They are not of the world, even as I am not of it. Sanctify them by the truth; your word is truth. *As you sent me into the world, I have sent them into the world.* For them I sanctify myself, that they too may be truly sanctified. (John 17:13–19 NIV, emphasis added)

There it is—no way around it. Our journey takes us right through Vanity Fair (the world)—and that is exactly where Jesus is sending us! But *why*?

Listen to our travelers' response. As the merchants were shouting, mocking, and ridiculing, demanding that the Pilgrims "buy" what the fair was "selling," Christian and Faithful offered a marvelous and challenging retort. They stated simply and powerfully, "We only buy the *Truth.*"

That declaration carries two profound realities. First, Christian and Faithful were able to recognize the distinction and the difference between the shabby "goods" the fair was selling from the authentic principles and precepts of what God has freely given us.

Their declaration also connotes that someone, somewhere, in that carnal carnival had a booth set up where only Truth, *real* Truth was being offered. It might not be the most visited stall at the fair. But curiosity seekers, skeptics, cynics, agnostics, atheists, secularists, and humanists would at least pass by the booth. Others might stop and quietly observe from afar. And yes, some would even linger long enough to really scrutinize and possibly accept what was being offered for free: Truth—absolute, unchanging, immutable. But someone has to "man the booth."

So let's go visit Vanity Fair together. We'll visit the booths and see for ourselves what is being bought and sold. Come and study the counterfeit goods being offered in the public square today so that you can better know how to offer the countervailing gift of Truth.

While we journey, let's remember the mandate that takes us right into the heart of the marketplace. It is concise and clear. The call is to *"Go and Tell,"* offering to anyone who will listen what we ourselves have been given. We will learn how to deliver that message in equal amounts of Truth and kindness. Will it be easy? Was it smooth sailing for Christian and Faithful? Bunyan writes that while the two Pilgrims behaved themselves so well, "taking their disgrace and shame with such meekness and patience, that several of the witnesses were won to their side," they were, nonetheless, thrown in jail.[2]

Judge Hategood would preside over their trial, and in the end Faithful would be executed. Bunyan writes, "Faithful died on the gallows, true to his convictions, sealing his testimony with his own blood."[3]

Most of us won't lose our lives when we venture into the marketplace of ideas, but it does remind us that this will be a challenging experience. Are you up for the challenge? Are you willing to go—when and where our Savior calls—even if it takes you out of your comfort zone and right into a lusty fair? If your answer is yes, then follow me!

In the morning of grace, when the Sun first arose,
And the Gospel divine put to flight all its foes,
The nations rejoiced, but forsook it so soon,
For the Sun in His strength was darkened at noon.

Light breaks at last! Hallelujah to God!
Darkness is past, let us shout it aloud:
From the mountains and hills let us gather the few
Who will stand for the right, and dare to be true.[4]

21

You shall leave everything loved most dearly,
and this is the shaft of which the bow of exile
shoots first. You shall prove how salt is the taste
of another man's bread and how hard is the
way up and down another man's stairs.

Dante, *Paradiso*

2
What, Me?
An Exile?

If you look up the word "exile" in the dictionary, you will find that the definition is "expulsion from one's native land by authoritative decree." In truth, no matter how you define it, being in exile is never a great place to be.

John Bunyan was exiled from his family while writing away in prison. His chief characters, Christian and Faithful, were also exiles in the strange land of Vanity Fair. Yet stories of exiles go back much further than Bedford, England.

It was the year 626 BC A young man from a landowning family received a divine call. Up to this point, young Jeremiah had lived a rather joyful life. He grew up in a household where God was not only honored but loved. He learned the law from his father, Hilkiah the priest.

As a young boy, Jeremiah had seen a profound reversal in the land of Judah. King Josiah had turned the nation back to God after his father, Amon, and grandfather, Manassah, had not only allowed but fostered widespread idol worship. But Josiah was a different kind of king who knew the results of repentance.

Enter young Jeremiah. God called him to a powerful but decidedly unpleasant ministry. Jeremiah's job was to remind the people of Judah of the terrible nature of sin. Think about that for a moment. Of all the work God might call us to, who would really, *truly* want the distasteful task of telling people, "You're in sin!" It's not a very popular message—yet it's a tremendously important one!

God takes sin seriously. The crucifixion of His only Son speaks directly to the deadly nature of sin. George MacDonald said, "Primarily, God is not bound to punish sin; He is bound to destroy sin. The only vengeance worth having on sin is to make the sinner himself its executioner."[1]

That was Jeremiah's job—to remind the people of Judah that they must be the executioners of sin in their own lives or face some grave consequences: destruction, captivity, and exile. What a message to be asked to deliver to a people who had reveled in sin for generations!

The nation of Judah had been drowning in a sea of decadence. Under King Manasseh, pagan worship had fallen to a new level of depravity. He dabbled in and allowed the practice of witchcraft; he consulted mediums; he sought out the advice of soothsayers; and worst of all, he participated in infanticide. King Manasseh had even sacrificed his own son to the Canaanite god Moloch.

What a horrible thought! History records that statues of Moloch were huge, with the head shaped to resemble a bull and outstretched, carved arms made ready for the sacrifice. Fires were built in the belly of the statues, and heat would radiate down the arms, waiting to cradle the child as he burned to death. On the dark days of the terrible deed, drums would beat and lutes would play loudly to drown out the cries of the children. Mothers stood by stoically, shedding no tear as a way of granting approval to the barbaric act. God's people had turned their back on Him—and a message of repentance was paramount for the salvation of the nation.

Being obedient to God has never been easy, and it wasn't for Jeremiah. Despite the fact that King Josiah had reversed some of the demonic practices of his relatives, Jeremiah knew it would be just a matter of time before the people of Judah would return to their pagan practices. God knew it too, and Jeremiah was tasked with declaring a prophetic message of repentance or punishment.

Isn't it interesting that Jeremiah (like so many of us) begins his journey by making excuses to the King of all creation for why he cannot possibly be qualified for what he is being asked to do? The Lord says that he has appointed—note that word—*appointed* Jeremiah to be a prophet. God is not asking Jeremiah's permission or dialoguing on the pros and cons of the job assignment. He is telling Jeremiah, after reminding him that He knew him even before he was a baby living under his mama's heart, that he was consecrated for service. God tells Jeremiah, "You *will* be a prophet," and Jeremiah responds by offering excuses for why that is not a good idea. "I do not know how to speak, for I am only a youth" (Jeremiah 1:6 ESV).

Being slow to anger, God reminded this teenager that He is in control. The question before Jeremiah was not one of age or eloquence—it was a question of obedience. It is the same question for each of us as well. Why do we so often engage in debate with God when He calls us out of our comfort zone and into a world where paganism and humanism are rampant?

Stop for a moment and ask yourself: The last time the Lord called me to do something for Him, what excuses did I offer up for not being obedient?

- Too old
- Too young
- Too busy
- Too married
- Too single
- Too rich
- Too poor
- Too educated
- Too uneducated

The list of excuses is endless. But God is patient and protective. He says to Jeremiah: "Do not say 'I am only a youth'; for to all to whom I send you, you shall go, and whatever I command you, you shall speak. Do not be afraid of them, for I am with you to deliver you, declares the Lord" (Jeremiah 1:7–8 ESV).

God then did something truly amazing. Jeremiah wrote that God put His hand out and touched the prophet's mouth, giving him the very words he would need for his calling. God literally touched the teenager on the lips!

As someone who has sat in front of a microphone for years, I *really* appreciate the fact that God can and does give us the very words we need to do the work He has called us to. Relying on His sovereign provision sure does take the pressure off, doesn't it?

So friend, whether or not *you* also sit in front of a microphone, we both need to be reminded that God always equips us for the work for which He calls us. When God calls us "out there," He will put the words "in here"—in our minds, in our hearts, and in our mouths. Obedience—not fear; that must be the Pilgrim's position of faith.

A CHALLENGING RESUME

It is not difficult to read about one of the major prophets of Scripture and think there must have been something supernatural about Jeremiah. But take just a moment to study his resume and ask yourself whether the prophet was unusual or whether our God is exceptionally gracious in selecting ordinary people for service to Him. He is, after all, the Creator of the universe. Does He really need us to do something for Him? Couldn't the Lord just as easily have painted a message in the sky that said simply to the people of Judah, "Repent or die"? His Word says that He could make seas part, turn water into blood, make serpents talk, and create a GPS out of a cloud—to name just a few miraculous acts. So does He need *us* to do something for Him? Or, as Dr. Henry Blackaby says, does He invite us to join Him "where (He) is already working"?[2]

God was working on the hearts of the people of Judah when Jeremiah was invited (granted, it was a decidedly clear and unambiguous invitation) to join Him in what He was about to do. As a result of Jeremiah's obedience, the prophet would be:

- Attacked by his brothers
- Beaten by a priest and put in stocks
- Publicly humiliated by a false prophet
- Put into prison by a king
- Threatened with death by government officials
- Thrown down into a cistern where he sank into the mud

Do you think Jeremiah might have run—*fast*—in the opposite direction if he had known ahead of time the price he would pay for obedience? I've thought about this quite a bit, and looking back on my own life, I have asked myself this very same question. Here's my answer—well, it's not *my* answer, but this teaching of A. W. Tozer clearly articulates *the answer* for me: "The true follower of Christ will not ask, 'If I embrace this truth, what will it cost me?' Rather he will say, 'This is truth. God help me to walk in it, let come what may!'"[3]

Jeremiah didn't look back—he looked forward. Obedience to God was more important than anything else. No matter what the cost, he went. He loved God more than he loved the world and into the world he went for the sake of the God he loved. That says it all. Sold out completely, totally, absolutely to God—that was Jeremiah. Unqualified, unexceptional, and unequivocally obedient—and the King of creation would use this teenager in a magnificent way!

Though there are very many nations all
over the earth . . . there are no more than two
kinds of human society, which we may justly call
two cities . . . one consisting of those who live
according to man, the other of those who
live according to God . . . To the City of Man
belong the enemies of God . . . so inflamed
with hatred against the City of God.

St. Augustine[1]

3
A Citizen of Two Worlds

Augustine lived in a period of history swirling with reform and dramatic change, a time that would leave an imprint on history for centuries to come. This great Christian expositor of Christian theology was raised in the North African area of Numidia in a city called Thagaste.

Augustine was raised in a household of conflict—his mother was a devout Christian, and his father was a committed pagan. This great apologist lived during the time just following the reforms of Constantine (AD 354–430). Even though Constantine had created an official Christian state, most of the population of the day would not be considered authentically Christian in their beliefs and practices.

Young Augustine had been sent to the best schools and showed an early acumen in scholastic work. He was given the job of Professor of Rhetoric in Carthage, a great commercial and political center on the bay of Tunis. But Augustine was a young man with a restless soul. He knew the teachings of Plato but longed for something more—something that would really feed his hungry heart and mind.

Like so many in the twenty-first century today, Augustine tried to fill the hole in his heart with all kinds of shabby goods. And just as so many choose to do in our present, postmodern world, the seeker sought out forbidden fruit. He followed the tradition of the day and became engaged to a woman, but quickly proved himself to be anything but a faithful husband-to-be.

Augustine was, in a word, a hedonist. He carried on a long-term affair with a woman, other than his fiancée, who bore him a son. Later, he would have another long-term affair with yet another woman.

While Augustine continued to feed his sexual appetite, his soul was starving. He joined with a group of friends who read, meditated, and pursued the ideals of philosophical truth. He wanted something more, something that truly satisfied his deepest longings. Augustine had a mind that embraced philosophy and a body that sought illicit embraces. He was the picture of a man in conflict.

The apostle Paul knew this same struggle. He, like Augustine, cried out, "For I know that nothing good dwells in me, that is, in my flesh. For I have the desire to do what is right, but not the ability to carry it out. For I do not do the good I want, but the evil I do not want is what I keep doing . . . Wretched man that I am! Who will deliver me from this body of death?" (Romans 7:18–19, 24 ESV).

History tells the story of a strange occurrence in the life of Augustine. One day, in the city of Milan, Italy, the hedonist was resting in a garden when he heard a child singing a little jingle. "Take and read, take and read," the child chanted.

Augustine turned to Paul's epistle to the Romans, the thirteenth chapter. He read, "Let us behave properly as in the day, not in carousing and drunkenness, not in sexual promiscuity and sensuality, not in strife and jealously. But put on the Lord Jesus Christ, and make no provision for the flesh in regard to its lusts" (Romans 13:13–14 NASB).

As if he had been struck by a bolt of lightning, Augustine was at once convicted and comforted. Here was what he had been searching for all along: transcendent Truth, piercing conviction, and eternal forgiveness. The hedonist became a true follower of Jesus Christ. And even though he protested his unworthiness, Augustine was appointed the Bishop of Hippo in AD 395.

In AD 410, the world was in tumult. The pagan Visigoths had been driven from their Germanic homeland by the Huns. As they pushed their way toward Rome, they butchered, plundered, and conquered any tribe that stood in their way. Much to the surprise of the Romans, the Visigoths could not be stopped, and Rome was sacked. For two hundred years that great capital city had known uninterrupted peace and tranquility. But now, things were markedly different.

Refugees from Rome poured into the cities of northern Africa, bringing with them stories of death and destruction. As Rome had been the seat of power for nearly the entire world, the stories were almost unimaginable to those who had grown up under the shadow of Roman domination.

Out of the cloud of geopolitical unrest rose a question pulling at the hearts of those who had known Rome at its zenith: Would Rome have fallen if it had not continued to worship the pagan gods? If the Christian God was real, why did He not protect them from the invading barbarians?

Augustine heard the roar of the questions and was convinced they needed answering. His response was penned in the classic work *City of God*. In his writings, we see the beginnings of post-first-century Christians struggling to define the relationship between the Church and the secular world around them. To use the words of John Bunyan: How do believers bound for the "Celestial City" navigate through a very earthly Vanity Fair?

Augustine identified two cities: the City of God and the City of Man. The City of God is the eternal kingdom of Jesus Christ, and the City of Man represents the temporal kingdoms, cultures, and societies of this life. While the two cities are decidedly different, Augustine believed the two cities were not completely cut off from each other. Knowing the Truth of Scripture, Augustine identified the City of Man as comprising both sinners and saints (those who have accepted the Lord as their Savior). The latter are bound for the Celestial City, and the former are bound for hell. But on earth, the two kingdoms are "mixed." For believers, our ultimate home is the City of God.

How then did Augustine define the interaction between the believer and the fallen world? He made his case on the basis of two verses of Scripture.

First, he cited in 1 Timothy: "I urge that supplications, prayers, intercessions, and thanksgivings be made for all people, for kings and all who are in high positions, that we may lead a peaceful and quiet life, godly and dignified in every way" (1 Timothy 2:1–2 ESV).

Augustine knew that even the unbeliever longed for a personal peace and that an external peace can bring calm and order to a society. It was the Christian's job, he wrote, to work toward maximizing peace, security, and social order in the culture. A personal life of peace fosters devotion to God and a deeper love for Him. Praying for our leaders helps them to rule wisely and, in turn, creates an atmosphere where the Church can flourish in an atmosphere of peace.

At the time Paul was teaching his young student Timothy, Christians were denied any role in governance in the Roman Empire. First, 1 Timothy 2:2 teaches the benefits of praying for both good leaders as well as bad ones. The early Church was instructed to pray even for Nero, a vicious persecutor of first-century Christians.

Augustine knew that even the unbeliever longed for a personal peace and that an external peace can bring calm and order to a society.

Second, Augustine referenced Jeremiah 29:7 where the children of God are told to "seek the welfare of the city where I have sent you into exile, and pray to the Lord on its behalf, for in its welfare you will find your welfare" (ESV).

The Bishop of Hippo brilliantly pointed out that the City of God and the City of Man were and *are*, for the present, "intermingled." He noted that, "as long as the two cities are intermingled we also make use of the peace of Babylon."[2] The phrase "The peace of Babylon" was defined by Augustine as, "the temporal peace of the meantime, which is shared by the good and bad alike."[3]

So how do we as Christians work for the "peace of Babylon"? Again, Augustine gives us a strong indication in *City of God*. He praised one emperor in particular who "never relaxed his endeavors to help the Church against the ungodly by just and compassionate legislation."[4] What does that mean? It means that when Christians bring a godly influence into the process of creating "just and compassionate legislation,"[5] we are, at the same time, working to protect and preserve the liberties of the Church to proclaim the Gospel of Jesus Christ.

Over 1,600 years ago, Augustine was able to discern between good leaders and bad leaders. While living in an era when neither he nor his contemporaries had the ability to actually elect earthly leaders, he knew what the Christian standard of good leadership was. He paints a powerful word picture of the "happy [just and good] ruler":

> We Christians call rulers happy, if they rule with justice; if amid the voices of exalted praise and reverent salutations of excessive humility, they are not inflated with pride, but remember that they are but men; if they put their power at the service of God's majesty, to extend His worship far and wide; if they fear God, love Him and worship Him; if more than their earthly kingdom, they love that realm where they do not fear to share the kingship . . . and if they do not fail to offer to their true God, as a sacrifice for their sins, the oblation, of humility, compassion and prayer.[6]

So check your passport, fellow Pilgrim. You will note that those of us who have trusted Jesus as our Lord and Savior have dual citizenship. We are citizens of a temporal kingdom, for the present, here on earth. But we are, more gloriously, citizens of heaven, *our real* home.

As we travel through this world, as both aliens and strangers, we must recognize the "intermingling" of the two kingdoms here on earth. We can't avoid or flee or shun the *temporary* kingdom and we mustn't— for the sake of the eternal kingdom to which we are bound.

Aim at heaven and you will get earth thrown in.
Aim at earth and you get neither.
C. S. Lewis[7]

All authority has been given to
Me in heaven and on earth.
Go therefore and make disciples
of all the nations, baptizing them
in the name of the Father and the Son
and the Holy Spirit.

Jesus
Matthew 28:18–19 NASB

4
Just Evangelize?

Are you ready to begin our exciting and challenging pilgrimage into Vanity Fair? Before we start our journey where we, like Christian and Faithful, will examine what is being bought and sold in the marketplace of ideas, we first must tackle the question, "Are we called *just* to evangelize?"

Those who argue against engaging the culture do so primarily by advancing the idea that the Great Commission necessarily keeps us out of the messy business of politics and public policy. And, at some level, they are right.

Politics does not work permanent change in the human heart. Public policy offers temporary solutions to some of the deep and profound issues humankind faces while citizens of this world. More importantly, a life transformed by the power of the Cross is a life that has been eternally revolutionized. Politics, in the final analysis, may change minds, but it does not change hearts or souls—only Jesus does.

Unfortunately, we have created, in many respects, a false choice. The argument advanced against engaging the world around us is this: Christians *either* work to win souls and "do the work of an evangelist" (2 Timothy 4:5 ESV) *or* we step into the marketplace and battle for Truth in the public square. We cannot do both. Or can we?

I came to know the Lord as my personal Savior when I was six years old. Blessed as I was, being raised in a Christian home, the love of the Lord and a love for His Word was all around me. I was immersed in a Christian environment. AWANA, Sunday school, mid-week Bible study, and Sunday night "sing-spirations" (I just dated myself, didn't I?) were regular activities for this gal.

One of the highlights of my teen years was going to church camp one week each summer. Nestled in the beautiful woods of northern Wisconsin, my church camp was a great place to play and grow spiritually. Each year, visiting missionaries would spend the week with us, challenging us to consider being used by God in fulfillment of the mandate of the Great Commission.

My heart would race as I heard stories about the Light of the World being taken into the dark corners of our earthly home. What could be more exciting than telling people how much they are loved by the King of all kings? Surely this had to be the greatest adventure anyone could experience! I would study and learn to love the words of Warren Wiersbe, the great Bible teacher, long after my time at camp had become warm memories. As I look back on those moments, some words of his summarize my heart perfectly: "You are a Christian because somebody cared. Now it's your turn."[1]

The apex of our week at camp was a ceremony held before a roaring bonfire on a Saturday night. If we felt, after a week of Bible study and personal reflection, the stirring of the Holy Spirit in our hearts, and sensed a desire to commit ourselves completely to Jesus, not just as Savior but as *Lord*, we were asked to publicly manifest that dedication to service by throwing a small stick on the bonfire. The burning of the wood was to represent a picture of a life consumed in service to Jesus—a willingness to go where He called, when He called, no matter what, no matter where.

I remember that Saturday night like it was yesterday. I couldn't wait to see where God would call me. What foreign country? What people group? What tribe? When, Lord? How soon can I leave? God would answer those questions several years later—and no one would be more surprised by His answers than this Pilgrim!

But before I share with you God's response to my request to serve Him, let me give you an example of how the Great Commission mandate *and* cultural engagement is not an either/or proposition. Rather, it is both!

Franklin Graham is the head of a marvelous international ministry known as the Samaritan's Purse. This ministry builds hospitals, provides disaster relief, and brings the Good News of the Gospel wherever they go. Franklin is a perfect example of the "both" response. Franklin is exemplary in his bold declaration of the Good News of the Gospel, like his father, Dr. Billy Graham. But he is equally willing to engage the culture *for* the cause of Christ.

Samaritan's Purse had been involved in humanitarian relief to war-torn Sudan long before any members of the Hollywood elite became publically aligned with the issue. More than two million Sudanese have been brutally butchered simply for who they are. Samaritan's Purse has worked to build hospitals, build satellite clinics, and provide clean drinking water and nutrition to starving families. In all of these deeds, those involved with the ministry have openly shared not only the Gospel of Jesus Christ but His love as well.

By the same token, Franklin has never been reticent about interacting with the culture. During one radio interview I had with him, Franklin encouraged all my listeners to write their representatives in Congress as well as members of the current administration. He boldly stated that unless the president of the United States (Bill Clinton at the time) "feels that the people are wanting [an end to slavery and genocide], and that the polls are demanding action, he will do nothing." Here was a minister of the Gospel challenging my audience to not only support a ministry that advances kingdom principles through word and deed but to engage the culture—the president of the United States and our elected officials—to do something to work against a pernicious evil. Evangelize or engage? For Franklin Graham there was no conflict. There shouldn't be for us either.

Being a Christian meant taking a Christian worldview out into the world, whether it was the halls of Congress or on a foreign mission field.

Elias Boudinot might not be a household name today, but he was very well known in the late 1700s. He served as president of the Continental Congress from 1782 to 1783. After that, he was elected to Congress, representing the state of New Jersey from 1790 to 1795. In 1817, following his tenure in government, Boudinot was selected to be president of the American Bible Society. Here was a man who took his Christianity into the public square, without hesitation. He saw the clarity in serving God in government just as clearly as he saw the mandate to spread the Gospel. For Boudinot, there was no choice between *either* evangelizing or engaging the culture. Being a Christian meant taking a Christian worldview out into the world, whether it was the halls of Congress or on a foreign mission field. He knew the power of the Word to change the world around us. He wrote:

> Hath God in his condescending grace appointed us to become his humble instruments in opening the eyes of the blind; in cheering the abodes of primeval darkness with the joyful sounds of redeeming love; in fulfilling the encouraging prophecy of the angel flying through the midst of heaven, having the everlasting Gospel in his hands, to preach to all nations, languages, tongues and people on the earth.[2]

But consider, if you will, this much older example of how there is no conflict between the call to evangelize and the mandate to engage the world around us by bringing Truth into the public square.

In Acts 16 we read of the illegal arrest of Paul because he dared to expose the charlatans in Philippi. A fortune-teller (or *psychic* in today's parlance) had been hot on the trail of Paul and his traveling partners.

The "psychic friend" wanted to draw customers away from the missionary and in the process gain new clients—a crafty and cunning scheme. But Paul exposed the phony racket for what it was, leaving a major negative impact on the economics of the fortune-telling trade (Acts 16:19). Money doesn't talk, it shouts.

The shouting reached the ears of the magistrate, who promptly threw Paul in jail, violating his rights as a Roman citizen. What was Paul doing that landed him in jail? He was preaching the Gospel of Jesus Christ—*evangelizing*. While in prison, Paul kept evangelizing (Acts 16:25–32). He was unashamed of the Good News that had so completely transformed him.

But when the time came for release from his illegal imprisonment, Paul refused to leave the jail. Instead, he called for the magistrates to come down to his prison cell and get a tutorial on false imprisonment. Listen to the strength of his words: "They have beaten us publically, uncondemned, men who are Roman citizens, and have thrown us into prison; and do they now throw us out secretly? No!" (Acts 16:37 ESV).

Just as Paul had preached the Gospel, he likewise desired to expose his unlawful imprisonment as well—in other words, cultural engagement. Why? Perhaps Paul sensed that his protesting might serve other Christians who would soon follow him at some future date in the Philippian jail. His protest might mean their protection.

Paul stood for Truth—the *broad truth* of the salvation afforded us by the work of the Cross and the *practical truth* regarding political corruption and illegal activity. For Paul, there was no conflict. It should be the same for us, as well.

The pages of history are rife with the stories of men and women whose relationship with Christ compelled them to go outside their comfort zone and into the world around them—not *just* to spread the Gospel and fulfill the Great Commission. They knew that the Jesus they preached was not just to be limited to the spiritual aspects of our future lives but that He was and is connected to the harsh realities of this life.

We are required to bring the whole Truth of the whole Gospel to the whole world. How do we do that without going right into the middle of Vanity Fair? By visiting that raucous marketplace, we Pilgrims are given the opportunity not only to share the elements of the Gospel message but to engage the very people we hope will join us for all eternity. William Booth, the founder and general of the Salvation Army, knew what it meant to go out into the world. His passion pours out of his words:

> While women weep, as they do now, I'll fight; while children go hungry, as they do now I'll fight; while men go to prison, in and out, in and out, as they do now, I'll fight; while there is a drunkard left, while there is a poor lost girl upon the streets, while there remains one dark soul without the light of God, I'll fight, I'll fight to the very end![3]

So, are you ready? Let's go visit the various booths that are set up in Vanity Fair. What *are* they selling? As the "merchants" shout at us, as they did to Christian and Faithful, will we pull the collars of our shirts up over our faces to hide who we are? Will we cringe in fear as they tell us to "buy, buy, *buy*"? Can we endure their taunts of "foreigner" and "stranger"? But, more importantly, will we respond, like the two travelers in Bunyan's tale, "We *only* buy the Truth"?

SECTION 2
Home Is Where the Heart Is— Or Should Be

The meaning of economic freedom is this:
that the individual is in a position to choose
the way in which he wants to integrate
himself into the totality of society.

Ludwig von Mises[1]

Do not wear yourself out to get rich;
do not trust your own cleverness.
Cast but a glance at riches, and they are
gone, for they will surely sprout wings
and fly off to the sky like an eagle.

Proverbs 23:4–5 NIV

5
A Living Letter to a Captive People

Money is such a ticklish subject, and given the headlines of the day, it's now a painful one as well. Look at the numbers. Unemployment has hovered above 8.5 percent for months.[2] Some financial experts say we may not see that number reduced for years.[3]

Each Thursday, the jobless claims come out. Week after week, we hear of hundreds of thousands of people who are searching for employment, trying to find jobs that simply aren't there. The Department of the Treasury has reported that America has accumulated more debt in the last few years than the total debt accrued under the first forty-one presidents combined.[4]

We are witnessing record-low mortgage rates and near-record lows in housing prices but given the generally pessimistic attitude toward the US economy, home prices are not only floundering—they are falling.

The numbers are staggering—almost too big to be completely understood. The debt has been increasing at about $4.27 billion per day. If you break that down, it means that nearly $53,000 of debt falls to each American household.[5] We are continually being reminded that we now live in the most perilous economic times since the Great Depression.

So what are the merchants doing about all the financial woe out there in Vanity Fair? For far too many years, we Pilgrims have been sold a bill of goods that tells us that if we just had more "stuff," we would be happier. How many times have you driven behind a car with a bumper sticker that declares, "He who dies with the most toys wins"? Nothing could be further from the truth. When we die, how many "toys" we accumulated in our lifetime will mean nothing. There are no U-Hauls being pulled by hearses. We come into this life empty-handed, and we leave the same way.

Yet, when traveling through the marketplace, we hear merchants shouting constantly to buy it *now*, with no money down. Far too many people have discovered that the pain of depression or loneliness can be temporarily removed by buying that new, shiny thing. We often forget that what we buy today, we end up paying for tomorrow—with *interest*.

A little more than 600 million credit cards are held by US consumers.[6] The average US household has $15,956.00 in debt spread over 3.5 credit cards.[7] Charles Dickens wrote with eloquence about spending and debt back in the 1800s, but his words are so apropos today: "Annual income twenty pounds, annual expenditure nineteen six, result happiness. Annual income twenty pounds, annual expenditure twenty pound ought and six, result misery."[8]

Over the last few years, we have watched the markets rise and fall, and fall still farther. For those who put their faith in Wall Street, there is now only a growing sense of instability and panic. There is no other way to put it: Our current economic situation is bordering on a global crisis.

Yet, as crushing as the numbers are for the US economy, what would it be like to struggle financially if you were a stranger in a foreign land—an exile? What if you were a captive living far from home? What if you lived in a place where the language, the customs, and the culture bore no resemblance to everything you knew and loved? How would you survive?

DEAR EXILES

The prophet Jeremiah was given the unenviable task of telling the people of Judah that, if they weren't watchful, they were going to turn back to the pagan worship of their forefathers. For forty years, Jeremiah preached a message of impending judgment and pleaded with the people to repent. But the people loved their idols more than they loved God—and judgment came. They willfully ignored the words of the Lord: "'Return, faithless Israel, declares the Lord. I will not look on you in anger, for I am merciful, declares the Lord; I will not be angry forever'" (Jeremiah 3:12 ESV).

But the people didn't return and they found themselves in captivity in a land far away from Judah.

Babylon was the jewel of the Near East. Located about fifty miles north of what is today's modern city of Baghdad, ancient Babylon was a huge pagan center. The translation of the city's name itself means "the gate of gods."

Babylon became a city of great importance to the trading network. Merchants brought their goods from as far away as India, Persia, and Egypt. Visitors marveled at the temples and the palaces. Among the pagan deity of Babylonia, Marduk was the king of the gods and the god of the rising sun. Legend tells the story that all the other Babylonian gods built the temple and the ziggurat to Marduk. The Tower of Babel was built in his honor.[9] Thriving, metropolitan, and pagan—that was Babylon in 597 BC. But for the Hebrew captives, it was not home.

King Nebuchadnezzar was a man who wanted to be remembered through the ages. History records that he ordered massive building projects, causing a flurry of architectural activity. In short order, the king made Babylon one of the seven wonders of the ancient world.[10] Herodotus, a Greek historian in 450 BC wrote, "Babylon surpasses in splendour any city in the known world."[11]

The walls surrounding the city were beautifully and painstakingly constructed with eight gates, including the striking Ishtar gate, measuring forty-seven feet in height and thirty-two feet in width. Today, that gate is on display in the Pergamon museum in Berlin, Germany.[12] The king built hanging gardens to comfort his homesick wife, creating an artificial mountain covered in plants to remind Amyitis of her homeland of Medes.[13] Trade increased and the city flourished. But it wasn't Jerusalem—and the people of Judah weren't there by choice. They were captives.

God never forgets His people—even when we are being held "captive" by our circumstances. The people of Judah had been warned but nonetheless had turned their backs on God. Punishment took the form of captivity, but still God kept watch over them.

Back in Judah, King Zedekiah sent emissaries on a mission to Babylon. The prophet Jeremiah took advantage of this and used the opportunity to send a letter of encouragement and instruction to the elders and the survivors of those who had been led into captivity in 597 BC.

God is not only holy, He is also very practical.

The letter may have been written by Jeremiah but the words were the words of the Lord of hosts, the God of Israel. The people were going to be in captivity for a very long time. Children would be born, grow old, and eventually die while in Babylon. God wanted them to know how to live in a place that wasn't really their home. God wants the same thing for us as well.

We live in a kind of captivity here on earth. The world is a fallen place, and we are so very far from the perfection we once knew in the garden but that time of perfection *will* come again. Someday all that was lost through sin will be regained in glory. But from this day until that moment when we dwell in His glorious presence, how then do we live in captivity?

God is not only holy, He is also very practical. Jeremiah's letter, found in chapter 29, offers us some very clear directives on how to not just live abundantly but to thrive while being a captive. Learning how to do what the Hebrews were instructed to do can help us learn how to do the same today.

But the twenty-ninth chapter of Jeremiah does something else. Taking to heart and applying the instructions for fruitful living found in the letter to the captives helps us more easily recognize bad ideas that advance bad choices with even worse consequences—ideas that are being bought and sold in the marketplace.

Jeremiah's letter serves as a road map as we navigate through Vanity Fair. It illuminates God's plan for us until we return home—to be with Him. It serves to prevent us from "buying" the shabby goods so readily for sale in Vanity Fair. The world offers one message—the Word offers another.

Our challenge is to learn to discern. God's Word continues to be a "light to our path" (Psalm 119:105 ESV). The Bible has been and always will be the lamp that breaks through the darkness of this life and helps us to arrive safely and securely at eternity. Let's study the letter and begin to discover how to live as a joyous captive!

> Feelings come and feelings go,
> And feelings are deceiving;
> My warrant is the Word of God—
> Naught else is worth believing.
>
> Though all my heart should feel condemned
> For want of some sweet token,
> There is One greater than my heart
> Whose Word cannot be broken.
>
> I'll trust in God's unchanging Word
> Till soul and body sever,
> For, though all things shall pass away,
> HIS WORD SHALL STAND FOREVER!
> Martin Luther[14]

There is no doubt that it is around the family
and the home that all the greatest virtues, the
most dominating virtues of human society,
are created, strengthened and maintained.

Winston Churchill[1]

Home is the bottom line of life, the anvil
upon which attitudes and convictions
are hammered out . . . the single most
influential force in our earthly existence.
No price tag can adequately reflect its value.

Charles Swindoll[2]

Build houses and settle down.

Jeremiah 29:5 NIV

6
There's No Place Like Home

Have you noticed how people will more often than not talk about their *home* when it involves people but will talk about their *house* when it entails work? We tend to consider home in terms of the people we live with—our parents, our siblings, and our children. A house is just a building, meaningless without the people who live there.

Jeremiah's letter contained very clear instructions to the Hebrews who, because of their disobedience, found themselves in captivity. They had been warned not to return to the pagan worship that had infiltrated the lives of their fathers and their forefathers. They watched a wicked king sacrifice his own child to a pagan god. They witnessed futile religions that demanded empty obedience with no love in return from a god who was not there. Nevertheless, they disobeyed and were taken off to a strange land and became the very definition of the word "stranger."

But our compassionate God, who loves us so consistently, wanted instructions given to the surviving elders, the priests, the prophets, and the people to know how to live while in captivity. Ten thousand Jews were about to get some real "insight for living" in Babylon. Jeremiah penned the words of the Lord; Elasah and Gemariah, two supporters of Jeremiah, delivered the instructions.

God's first instruction was clear and straightforward. "Build houses and live in them" (Jeremiah 29:5 NASB). The directive served as a wake-up call. The instruction to build homes meant that the Hebrews were going to be in Babylon a long, long time. It would have been so easy for them to slip into despair and to sink deep into depression. But God wanted His children to live, *really live,* even though they were strangers and aliens. Building a home and living in it was a concrete way of settling down and settling in. They were to put down roots.

Given the current economic situation in America, it has become harder and harder for people to buy a home or to sell the house they currently have and move into one that better fits their needs. But whether we own or rent, where we live right *now* is our home. Knowing that our real home is with Him in heaven, how can we honor and glorify Him, right now, with our temporary homes on earth? By the way, when you think about it, there is a mansion currently under construction for us in glory—with no mortgage! Does it get any better than that?

The world has an interesting take on the idea of home building. Part of the financial pain we are feeling now is directly attributable to the greed that has permeated our culture. *Bigger is better* became the lifestyle for the twentieth century. Housing lenders began changing the way mortgages were granted. No longer did buyers have to provide income verification nor did they have to put down 20 percent of the purchase price—safeguards that, until recently, were common qualifications for most home buyers. Suddenly, families making $35,000 a year were able to purchase $750,000 homes. Why? It turns out, behind the scene, some in the banking world were pocketing big profits. Contrary to the famous line out of the movie *Wall Street,* "Greed is [not] good." In short order, America would be paying for this greed in a big way.

During the apex of the housing boom, a new term emerged: *McMansions.* The word made reference to giant homes that were quickly constructed but were not necessarily well made. The idea was to take the design of a big house and make it even bigger. After all, hadn't the merchants in Vanity Fair been selling the concept that bigger is better? And, unfortunately, some consumers were "buying" into it.

After the housing market fell through the basement, these McMansions were extremely difficult to sell, since no one had the money. Or, if they did sell, they sold at an average of 33 percent below the original purchase price.[3] Ouch! Bigger is not necessarily better, and bigger can certainly cost much more in the long run.

Bigger is not necessarily better, and bigger can certainly cost much more in the long run.

God instructed the captives to "build houses and live in them." He didn't discuss how big the houses had to be. Rather the instruction was given to the captives to build homes as a way of preparing for a long captivity. But while in Babylon, their homes would be a way of building up their families and preparing for the future.

HOUSE BEAUTIFUL

They say that "confession is good for the soul." If that is true, here is a little admission I would like to make. For the longest time, I was under the mistaken idea that "hospitality" was a special gifting from the Lord. And, truth be told, I was very glad I didn't have the gift! Why?

I am a typical firstborn child. Whatever I do, I always think I need to do it with twenty-five extra-credit points. That becomes particularly onerous when it comes to hospitality. If my home wasn't *perfectly* decorated, with all the rooms *perfectly* cleaned, and all the food *perfectly* prepared, I would be *perfectly* miserable while entertaining. After all, didn't everything have to be *perfect* for me to be hospitable?

When all else fails, read the instructions. Eventually I decided I really needed to find out what God had to say on the subject of using our homes to be hospitable. What I discovered was stunning and challenging. Romans 12:13 clearly states: "Practice hospitality" (NIV). That's it. Pure, simple, and clear. Not a gift—a directive.

This verse radically changed my thinking on how we are to use our homes to honor God and convey His love to all who enter. The world merchants are trying to get us to buy the biggest house we can, as a status symbol of success, while God is asking us to use our homes, regardless of the size, to manifest hospitality.

Realizing that our King is asking us to be hospitable, how exactly do we do this?

For starters, don't think everything has to be perfect! That might be obvious to some of us, but to others, like me, we have to get to the place where we live our lives with open hands and open hearts. If we are willing to offer up to Him all that we have, including our kitchens and our living rooms, He is both pleased and honored.

According to one statistic, 29 percent of Americans ages eighteen to twenty-four do not even know who lives next door.

When God directed His children, through the prophet Jeremiah, to build houses while in captivity, He knew this would be an opportunity for His people to show to others the unconditional love that they (and we) had been given. The same holds true today.

What kind of a relationship do you have with your neighbors—and not just the ones you like or get along with but *all* your neighbors? Do you know the people who live on your street or in your apartment building? That might seem like a strange question but with all the social media available today (an ironic term here), we are less social than we have ever been before. According to one statistic, 29 percent of Americans ages eighteen to twenty-four do not even know who lives next door.[4]

We may be quick to post our latest adventure on Facebook or tweet a friend about some humorous story, but what about inviting a neighbor in for a hot meal or a cup of coffee? As captives in Babylon, our homes can become a mission field to those who do not yet know Jesus, the Messiah.

Every year at Christmas, I make bread for all of my neighbors. I arrange it in a pretty basket and always include a card that shares the real meaning of Christmas. My husband and I then go door-to-door, dropping off the baskets and spending a few minutes chatting with those who live on our street. Some of my neighbors look forward to our bread basket every year; others never say a word. Regardless, this simple act is a way for us to convey to others the love of Christ—and it helps me to learn obedience and causes me to step outside of my comfort zone by practicing hospitality.

Is there a spare room in your house that can help a young woman in the midst of a crisis pregnancy? Do you know of someone in your neighborhood who is ill or elderly and could use a good house cleaning? How about cutting the grass for that single mom across the street or walking the dog of a neighbor who pretty much keeps to himself (the neighbor keeps to himself, not the dog!)? If we are going to be honest with one another, there really is no shortage of opportunities for us to "practice hospitality."

The merchants in Vanity Fair continue to shout that "me" is the center of the universe. "You deserve a break today" and "You're worth it" are catchphrases used by Madison Avenue to get us to buy a product. We stand in the checkout line at the grocery store and see magazines with titles like *Self* and *Us*. But being a captive in a hostile, fallen world means we recognize that living really isn't about "me." It's about Him. Showing His love through "building homes" in Babylon is not only countercultural, it is practical, applied Christianity.

Jeremiah was directed by God to tell the Hebrew people that, regardless of whether they were in their homeland or not, they were to put down roots and build homes and live in them.

G. K. Chesterton once wrote, "We make our friends; we make our enemies, but God makes our next-door neighbor."[5] God was giving His people an opportunity for service (and for personal growth) by directing them to let the people of Babylon know that what mattered most wasn't their mailing address but the responsive, obedient condition of their hearts. Captive people can still be obedient people.

You and I don't belong here. Our home is with Him—and someday we will take up permanent residency with our great King. But for now, while we're living in a strange land, let's seize the moment and let our lights shine in the dark world of our own neighborhoods.

God writes the Gospel not in the Bible alone,
but on trees and flowers and clouds and stars.

Unknown—attributed to Martin Luther

Adam was a gardener, and God, who made him, sees
that half of all good gardening is done upon the knees.

Rudyard Kipling[1]

Plant gardens and eat what they produce.

Jeremiah 29:5 NIV

7
Harvesting from and for Heaven

When the tinker from Bedford penned his classic *Pilgrim's Progress* from his prison cell, he took his readers not only into the lusty market-place known as Vanity Fair but he also had them travel the highways and byways of the Christian experience.

Bunyan, like Jesus, knew that we would struggle with the issue of money. There are more than 1,600 verses in Scripture that mention money, which leads us to the conclusion that God knew that the challenges of materialism and money management would know no limits by time or culture. Money is both a blessing and a challenge.

In Bunyan's book, he writes that Christian and Hopeful had entered a town called Fair-speech. Hopeful asks his traveling companion about the town, and Christian cautions that it is not a place where they want to get detained. He goes so far as to tell Hopeful to "keep moving."

As the pair draws closer to the city, they become aware of a man named Demas, who is vigorously waving his arms and calling out to them in a loud voice. "Hello!" he shouted, smiling broadly. "Over here! This way, my friends! I have something to show you!"

Bunyan writes:

CHRISTIAN: *What can you show us that is important enough to turn us out of our way?*
DEMAS: *Here is a silver mine, and people digging in it for riches. If you will come, you will see that you can by a little effort provide yourselves with great wealth.*
     "Let us go and see," said Hopeful.
CHRISTIAN: *Not I. I have heard of this place and of many who have lost their lives there. Besides, that treasure is a snare to those who get it; it tarnishes, and cankers, and poisons one's body and mind.*
     Then Christian called to Demas, "Is not the place dangerous? Has it not been the cause of the wrecking and ending of many pilgrimages?"
     "No, not very dangerous," Demas said with tongue in cheek, "except to those who are careless."
     Then said Christian to Hopeful, "Let us not take one step in that direction, but keep straight on our way."[2]

Brilliant biblical insight! Bunyan, who knew for himself the weight of poverty, knew also that the world offered a tempting message about the allure of materialism and wealth. The world tells us to simply line our pockets with "silver" and we will waltz into a world of happiness. But Bunyan knew that was a false and dangerous message.

No character in *Pilgrim's Progress* is named without a purpose. Consider the name "Demas." Bunyan used a bit of creative and purposely pointed writing by picking that name. Consider this. Demas is named in the New Testament as a traveling companion to the apostle Paul. What a joy that would have been! This great former persecutor, who had a blinding encounter with the Savior, was now traveling the world to teach anyone who would listen about salvation by grace and grace alone.

But somewhere along the roads of the Middle East, Demas began to change. Paul writes in his second letter to Timothy, "For Demas, because he loved this world, has deserted me" (2 Timothy 4:10 NIV). Paul doesn't expand on what happened or give specifics, but the phrase *loved this world* gives a fairly strong hint that Demas had been infected by the love of money.

Money had literally taken Demas off the path of service and missions. He wasn't the first to experience this lust, and he won't be the last. Jesus talked about our difficult relationship with money by painting the unforgettable word picture of a camel going through the eye of needle as being easier than a wealthy man entering into heaven. Having seen both a camel and a needle, I can tell you, that *is* tough!

Paul, still teaching his young student Timothy, writes that, "The *love* of money is a root of all kinds of evil" (1 Timothy 6:10 ESV, emphasis added), and he goes on to further the point by adding, "Some people, eager for money, have wandered from the faith and pierced themselves with many griefs" (1 Timothy 6:10 NIV). John Wesley understood this reality when he said, "When I have money, I get rid of it quickly, lest it find a way into my heart."

DEAR EXILE, NEXT INSTRUCTION

God loves gardens, as evidenced by the way they weave their way through Scripture.

Let's return now to Babylon, back into captivity. Jeremiah, by way of emissaries from King Zedekiah, has a letter of instructions sent to the captives. Jeremiah pens the letter, but he is really taking dictation from the Lord (Jeremiah 24:5).

God wanted His people to know how they are not only to *live* but to *thrive* while so far from their home in Judah. He has told them first to build their homes and to live in them. But now, He commands them to do something else: "Plant gardens and eat their produce" (Jeremiah 29:5 ESV).

How absolutely fascinating that the God of all creation would instruct the Israelites to plant gardens! Why would He instruct people who are going to live in a foreign land for seventy years to plant gardens and eat what they produce?

God loves gardens, as evidenced by the way they weave their way through Scripture. Adam and Eve are given the task of tending a garden of perfection. Sin makes its first appearance in a garden. The Bible mentions gardens that grow herbs, spices, fruit trees, and cucumbers. We read of gardens that are enclosed, some refreshed by fountains; gardens used for burials, for idol worship, for retirement, and for entertainment.

Jesus pours out His heart to His Father and ultimately surrenders to the will of His father in a garden. We read of the garden with the Tree of Life in Genesis, and we find it again in the book of Revelation. Gardens are important to God.

I will never forget the opportunity my husband, Craig, and I had to meet HRH the Prince of Wales and to visit his home at Highgrove. Prince Charles has long been known for his love of gardening, and we had been invited to view his efforts with organic farming.

The heir to the British throne is seen as quite a successful watercolorist and that same use of color can be found in all the gardens that make up what is called "The Garden at Highgrove." It is not one garden, but a composite of some of the most exquisite and perfectly cared for gardens in the world. There is the Sundial Garden with its beautiful yew hedge; the Terrace Garden that leads toward the Thyme walk; the statues of the goddesses representing the four seasons; the Cottage Garden, resembling something out of *Alice in Wonderland*; the Wild Flower Meadow and Woodland Garden with their bright, explosive primary colors and Moorish arch of Cotswold stone. But most memorable to me personally was the Sanctuary, a structure nestled in the back of one of the gardens, built in 1999 to commemorate the millennium and as a thanksgiving to God. I have seen the magnificent gardens of an earthly prince, and now I can only imagine what the gardens of the King of all kings must be like. I can't wait to see them!

God tells His children to plant gardens—and eat their produce. Why?

We have created economic chaos in our country today where the "haves" and "have-nots" have become the "wants" and "will nots."

God is so many things, not the least of which is practical. We are commanded to be *practical* in our earthly work, applying ourselves to the task of providing for our families. Going back again to the apostle Paul, we read what was written to the believers at Thessalonica, but still applies to us today. We are told to "attend to your own business and work with your hands, just as we commanded you, so that you may behave properly toward outsiders and not be in any need" (1 Thessalonians 4:11–12 NASB). God's principle applies to both the captives in Babylon as well as the church at Thessalonica. It applies to us today, as well.

Our culture shouts at us, like Demas calling to Christian and Hopeful, that to be happy, we must be rich. Or the merchants cry out to us the opposite message: "Let someone else pay the bill; why provide for your family by the efforts of your *own* hands?" We have created economic chaos in our country today where the "haves" and "have-nots" have become the "wants" and "will nots." Paul tells us (and Timothy) that, "If anyone does not provide for his own, and especially for those of his household, he has denied the faith and is worse than an unbeliever" (1 Timothy 5:8 NASB).

God had priorities for the Israelites and required that they work, produce, and provide. And He has priorities for us too. He requires that we seek Him first. "Seek first His kingdom and His righteousness, and all these things will be added to you" (Matthew 6:33 NASB). The people of Judah had not heeded the warnings of Jeremiah and had turned their backs on God. The result was bondage—for seventy years.

Gardening and harvesting go together. Anyone who has ever worked on a farm or planted a vegetable garden knows the hard work of planting, watering, fertilizing, and harvesting. As we "tend our gardens" while captives here on earth, how do we practice *the principle of the harvest*?

We often hear of the concept of "reaping what we sow," and more often than not, we tend to think of that only in negative terms—as in receiving the negative consequences of our own wrong choices. But turn that around for a moment and consider that it might also mean that what we do for the Lord, with our lives and with our finances, can bring about a positive blessing as well.

The principle of the harvest means not only giving to our families but giving back to the Lord as well. Statistics reveal that about one in ten Christians gives regularly to the Lord.[3] That gives the idea of "giving one tenth" a whole different meaning! God tells us to "plant our financial garden" and when the "harvest" comes in, we are to give back to Him, *cheerfully!*

In addition, we must plan. "Each one must do just as he has purposed in his heart" (2 Corinthians 9:7 NASB). All around us is evidence that life is getting more complex, allowing less time for planning. But we captives need to plan for the "garden" we will plant, plan for the time of the "harvest," and plan for the use of the "fruit" from our garden. Without planning, our families will not be provided for, we become a burden to others, and giving back to the Lord simply will not happen.

Attitude is important when being both a captive and a gardener. Work is a blessing, not a chore. You might not currently have the greatest or most interesting job, but it's harder to be the person who has no job at all. God refused to allow His people to be sullen or lazy while living as captives. He told them, quite literally, *to get to work.* Plant and eat. Don't plant—and you won't eat!

The economic disaster of 2008 served as a wake-up call that, with relative ease, "famine" can occur. But history is littered with stories of famines. Consider what took place in AD 46. Because of the poor harvests that took place under the rule of Emperor Claudius, Judea experienced severe famine. Enter a relatively unknown Christian prophet named Agabus. We are introduced to him in Acts: "One of them named Agabus stood up and began to indicate by the Spirit that there would certainly be a great famine all over the world. And this took place in the reign of Claudius" (Acts 11:28 NASB).

So how did the Church respond to this gloom and doom report? "And in the proportion that any of the disciples had means, each of them determined to send a contribution for the relief of the brethren living in Judea. And this they did, sending it in charge of Barnabas and Saul to the elders" (Acts 11:29–30 NASB). The believers responded, not by hoarding and panic. Rather, they surveyed where the need was and acted accordingly.

Jerusalem was the hardest hit by the famine. The Church responded by helping out financially. Antioch sent some financial assistance, and Paul advised the believers in Corinth to do the same. Some of the early churches gave, and some did not, proving that there really is nothing new under the sun. Disparity in giving in the Church is as commonplace today as it was in the first century.

But the church at Philippi was different. Those believers gave regularly and gave happily to Paul's ministry—and they did so again and again. Part of the harvest from the gardens we plant during "captivity" is to go directly to the work of the Church, whether or not the culture is under the weight of famine. The world says, "Me first!" but the Word says, "God first!" May we always put that principle into action.

Plant your gardens—and be good stewards of the harvest. Plan, plant, and prepare. We may be living in "captivity" today as believers, but we can still, as Pilgrims longing for our *real* home, enjoy the abundance of the heart that comes from obedience. Obedience always leaves us so completely satisfied—and never "hungry" for what the world has to offer. When the world shouts at us to fear and hold tight because of the financial famine in the land, we have a tremendous opportunity to live counterculturally by giving—faithfully. The Babylonians must have been amazed to see the people they had captured, from a far away land, put down roots and get to work tending their gardens. What a way to convey complete and total trust in the God of glory!

Captivity was never designed to be fun or exciting. It is hard work in the midst of very unpleasant circumstances. But just as God provided for the Israelites, He will provide for us today as well.

The amount of money we may have in the bank, or tucked under the mattresses, pales in comparison to the unlimited supply of His sufficient grace. Planting our hearts in the firm, rich soil of His Truth can yield a harvest of opportunities for each of us—an opportunity to be found faithful, even while being held captive in a financially fearful world.

Now—go plant your garden!

SECTION 3

Marriage, Monogamy, Miracles, and Mistakes

Marriage is the mother of the world. It preserves kingdoms, and fills cities and churches, and heaven itself.

Jeremy Taylor[1]

[Matrimony] was ordained for a remedy and to increase
the world and for the man to help the woman and the
woman the man, with all love and kindness.

William Tyndale[2]

Marry and have sons and daughters;
find wives for your sons and give
your daughters in marriage.

Jeremiah 29:6 NIV

8
I Do, I Did, I Will

Welcome to one of the busiest and noisiest sections of Vanity Fair. Let's stop and linger for a while as we examine the "goods" being bought and sold over the ideas of love and marriage. We will have to push our way through the crowds gathered around the "booth" for one very obvious reason: Who doesn't want to be loved?

Television programs, movies, and books written about love saturate our culture. Countless novels, adorned with portraits of shirtless men, can be purchased in the same stores where we buy our eggs and milk. And, as we approach the checkout line, we glance over and see racks of magazines with cover stories reporting the latest torrid Hollywood affairs. On our way home from the store, we spot the movie marquee

If the entire concept of marriage was defined and designed by Him—why is it sometimes so difficult?

and see titles like *Sex in the City*, the *Twilight Saga*, and *Crazy Stupid Love*. Every single one of us desires to be loved—madly, deeply, unconditionally by *someone*. Sadly, we are often "sold" some pretty shabby stuff that looks like "love" but in truth is a cheap imitation of the real thing.

God is the author not only of *real* love but of marriage. It is often said that the Bible is a book that both begins and ends with a marriage. So why is marriage so dear to His heart? And why does it appear so early on in His Word? And, if the entire concept of marriage was defined and designed by Him—why is it sometimes so difficult?

Let's start with the "instituting" of the institution of marriage. Genesis chapter 1 records how the world was made, gloriously, mysteriously, and perfectly. We read of the beginning of day and night, water and land, fish and birds. God lets us stand back and marvel at His handiwork. He is the *great* Creator; He not only paints the world with color, but He Himself designs the colors!

Then the King speaks to all generations and says, "'Let us make man in *our* image, after *our* likeness'" (Genesis 1:26 ESV, emphasis added). In one short, yet profound verse, we get our first lesson about the triune nature of God. But something else happens in this passage. We learn that we—mere mortals, specks of dust on planet Earth—are made in *His* image. Stop right now and think about that. God doesn't say this about the "great sea creatures," nor does He make this declaration about any one of the "living creatures that move." He only says it about us—human beings. We are the crown jewel in His created world. We have a place in His heart that nothing else can occupy.

After each day of creation, God declared it to be "good." But it is only after He makes man that God says, "It is *not* good . . ." He is not saying that the first human He created was wrong or somehow broken. But the gracious Creator is remarking on the state of "aloneness" of this first human. The man needs something more, something to complete him—*or someone*. This man, Adam, needs a helper, a companion, a friend. Recognizing the void, God fills it. "I will make him a helper fit for him" (Genesis 2:18 ESV). God fills the missing space, with a perfect response, and He does it majestically!

In Genesis chapter 2, we read of the first surgery. A deep sleep overcomes Adam (imagine, no anesthesia!) and while he's under God's scalpel, a rib is removed from Adam's side. But the surgery doesn't end there. In place of the missing rib, God caused flesh to grow over that area of Adam's torso. Orthopedic surgery followed by plastic surgery followed by—*a woman*! Even the name of this new creation is tied inexorably to the man Adam: "This *at last* is bone of my bones and flesh of my flesh; she shall be called Woman, because she was taken out of Man," Genesis 2:23 (ESV, emphasis added).

"At last!" This always makes me laugh out loud. Do you think Adam was longing, maybe even panting, for a companion? Here he is in a garden—a perfect place, freshly made by the hand of God Himself. Adam had a feast for the eyes, the divinely appointed job of gardener, and direct communication with God. But there was a missing piece. Adam's "hole in the heart" was God-designed—and God Himself knew just how to fill the void—and fill it He did!

Adam is given the privilege of naming this new being—and he picks the word *Woman*. In Hebrew, the word is *isha*. But maybe what Adam really said was, *"Whoa*, man"! when he first saw her, which was later translated into "woman!" I jest, but there is no joking that Adam waited and wanted and needed a woman.

Here is an important point to consider as we linger in the market-place, and it is a much-disputed idea in a postmodern world. Note the way in which the first human beings were created: "For man was not made from woman, but woman from man. Neither was man created for woman, but woman for man" (1 Corinthians 11:8–9 ESV).

That passage is sure to make the feminists angry. Yet it is not only historical fact, it is also biblical Truth. So it raises the question of *why*? Why was woman made from man and not the other way around? Is woman deemed inferior to man? It is worth pointing out that God made the woman Eve out of the "side" of Adam. She wasn't made from his foot, so he could stomp on her; not from his head, so he could intellectualize his relationship with her; but out of his rib, the spot closest to his heart, so that they might, together, serve God side by side. In His infinite sovereignty, God choose to make man out of the dust of the earth. But He made woman out of the man—which takes us directly to the establishment of the first great institution, marriage.

'TIL DEATH DO US PART

Who doesn't love a wedding? Television is peppered with programs that give a strong hint that our modern-day TV consumers want to watch anything that has to do with weddings. *Say Yes to the Dress* and *Bridezillas*, along with specials like *Kim Kardashian's Wedding* and the wedding of rock band KISS member Gene Simmons on *Gene Simmons Family Jewels* score high ratings consistently with audience members. We are the invited voyeurs to these ceremonies, and we don't even have to come with a gift for the happy couple.

But how many television shows celebrate not the wedding but the marriage? If we use the metric of TV as an indicator of what the world thinks about this topic, we can see how Hollywood portrays this God-designed institution:

Married with Children (Dad is a buffoon; children are horrifically disrespectful)
Desperate Housewives (all adultery—*all* the time)
Trading Spouses (no explanation needed here!)
Sister Wives (viewers get an up-close-and-personal tutorial on polygamy)

This is just a small sampling of what's on television. No wonder we, as a culture, are so confused about what the institution of marriage is all about!

So why *did* God create and establish the institution of marriage? Couldn't Adam and Eve simply have continued tending their garden and naming the animals? God's Word pushes us deeper, telling us there is something more here—some greater meaning that underscores just how much we are loved by our Creator.

Genesis goes on to say, "Therefore a man shall leave his father and his mother and hold fast to his *wife*, and they shall become one flesh" (2:24 ESV, emphasis added). *The two shall become one.* Think about that for a moment. The Bible is not simply referring to the intimate act of sexual

Out of His love for us, God uses this model, this oneness, as a magnificent way of letting us know just how much He loves us.

expression but this "oneness" exemplifies and underscores that unconditional love must necessitate giving up a part of "me" in marriage. One can't be two. *One* means part of the husband and part of the wife creating a new whole, this union called marriage.

Paul refers to this in Ephesians as "a profound mystery" (Ephesians 5:32 NIV). The Greek word *mysterion* means something is so important and so special that we can only really obtain its meaning through the instruction of the Holy Spirit. In other words, "Pay attention here, this is big!"

Out of His love for us, God uses this model, this oneness, as a magnificent way of letting us know just how much He loves us. Paul helps us along in our understanding by saying immediately after the "pay attention part" that, "I am saying that it refers to Christ and the church" (Ephesians 5:32 ESV) and here is the explanation: "Wives, submit to your own husbands, as to the Lord. For the husband is the head of the wife even as Christ is the head of the church, his body, and is himself its Savior. Now as the church submits to Christ, so also wives should submit in everything to their husbands" (Ephesians 5:22–24 ESV).

I can hear the loud groan coming from the marketplace as I write this. The merchants of Vanity Fair simply don't get this, and frankly, sometimes we don't either.

When the debates for the Republican nomination were being televised during the 2008 presidential campaign, Governor Mike Huckabee was asked by the moderator what we often refer to as a "gotcha" question. Carl Cameron of Fox News wanted to know why Governor Huckabee had allowed his name, along with several dozen others, to be used in a full-page ad in the *New York Times*. The ad was placed by the Southern Baptist Convention, and its purpose was to declare the primacy and definition of marriage as God designed it. Part of the copy stated, "A wife is to submit herself graciously to the servant leadership of her husband."

Cameron, after reading aloud that portion of the ad, went on to ask Huckabee if having his name included with the other names was a "politically viable position" for a general election in 2008. Huckabee's answer was not only fabulous but eloquent:

> You know, it's interesting: Everybody says religion is off limits, except we always can ask me the religious questions. So let me try to do my best to answer it.
> (APPLAUSE)
> And if we're really going to have a religious service, I'd really feel more comfortable if I could pass the plates, because our campaign could use the money tonight, Carl.
> (LAUGHTER AND APPLAUSE)
> We'll just go all the way.
> First of all, if anybody knows my wife, I don't think they for one minute think that she's going to just sit by and let me do whatever I want to. That would be an absolute total misunderstanding of Janet Huckabee.
> The whole context of that passage—and, by the way, it really was spoken to believers, to Christian believers. I'm not the least bit ashamed of my faith or the doctrines of it. I don't try to impose that as a governor and I wouldn't impose it as a president.
> But I certainly am going to practice it unashamedly, whether I'm a president or whether I'm not a president. But the point . . .
> (APPLAUSE)
> . . . the point, and it comes from a passage of scripture in the New Testament book of Ephesians, is that as wives submit themselves to the husbands, the husbands also submit themselves, and it's not a matter of one being somehow superior over the other. It's both mutually showing their affection and submission as unto the Lord.
> So, with all due respect, it has nothing to do with presidency. I just wanted to clear up that little doctrinal quirk there, so that

2048

there's nobody who misunderstands that it's really about doing what a marriage ought to do—and that marriage is not a 50/50 deal, where each partner gives 50 percent.

Biblically, marriage is 100/100 deal. Each partner gives 100 percent of their devotion to the other and that's why marriage is an important institution, because it teaches us how to love.

Mike Huckabee, you may recall, is not only the former governor of Arkansas, a presidential contender of 2008, and a TV host, but he is also an ordained pastor. With his usual wit and kindness, the governor gave a condensed sermon on national television on the passage of Ephesians 5, describing the plan and purpose for marriage. What was meant as a political landmine ending up being a great witness for the Truth of God's Word.

The governor was spot on. Marriage is a paradigm, a model, a word picture of the clarion call for wives to submit to the headship of their husbands because Christ is the head of the Church. Likewise—and this is the part the world always misses, husbands must *also* submit to Christ, in accordance with His role as Savior and Lord. In other words, there is a whole lot of submitting going on—and the world gags on the concept of submission!

In an "I am woman, hear me roar" kind of a world, submission doesn't play very well. Just like the idea of being a "self-made man" doesn't jell with the idea of submitting to a higher authority. But the world gets confused on this issue of submission, not realizing that, for the believer, submission does not mean failure or some kind of modern-day slavery. Rather, submission means victory! Real freedom comes from surrendering to Christ as King. What liberty we find in knowing that He is in charge, and we are not; that He is God, and we are not. What protection there is in knowing how much He loves us—to the point that He made the ultimate sacrifice! God designed and instituted marriage so we would see and know through the ages how much He cares for us. Marriage is not *just* about a man and a woman falling in love and wanting to live "happily ever after." The profundity of this institution is the continual reminder that Christ so loved *us* that He submitted to the will of His Father and gave His life for *us*. Perfect love—perfectly manifested—perfectly pictured in the model of marriage.

William Barclay stated this idea superbly when he said:

> Even after he has stressed the subordination of women, Paul goes on to stress even more directly the essential partnership of man and woman. Neither can live without the other. If there is subordination, it is in order that the partnership may be more fruitful and more lovely for both.[3]

Marriage was not a concept created by government. It wasn't an idea thought up by Hollywood writers or by romance novelists. It began in the heart and mind of God, even before sin came into the world. It is both practical and profound. It provides comfort, creates children, offers companionship, and continually conveys the unconditional and sacrificial love Christ has for us. It is no wonder marriage is under attack.

The "Great Deceiver" wants to do all within his power to destroy marriage.

Having looked at marriage through the "eyes" of the One who created it, are you ready to walk around Vanity Fair and see what the merchants are shouting? Prepare yourself: It's not going to be pretty. But understanding that this institution created in the garden of Eden has everything to do with the Lordship of Jesus Christ, we can better understand why the "Great Deceiver" wants to do all within his power to destroy marriage. Oh, and you'd better put on *all* your protective armor. You are going to need every bit of it.

Marriage is a wonderful institution,
but who wants to live in an institution?

Groucho Marx

God's great cosmic joke on the human race was requir-
ing that men and women live together in marriage.

Mark Twain

Enjoy life with the wife whom you love,
all the days of your vain life that
he has given you under the sun.

Ecclesiastes 9:9 ESV

9
What God Has Joined Together

Someone once said, "Marriage is not a word, it is a sentence." If that is true, then more and more Americans are speechless. According to a November 2010 poll released by the Pew Research Center, traditional marriage is on the decline. In 2008, about half of the adults in this nation were married compared to 1960 when seven in ten were.[1]

Working in conjunction with *Time* magazine, the Pew nationwide survey discovered what they are calling a "marriage gap." Their survey showed that adults with a college education and a good income are more likely to marry than those who are on a lower rung of the socio-economic ladder.

The survey found that those with a high school diploma or less are just as likely to say they *want* to marry as those who have a college degree. But for those with less education, a far higher premium was placed on the idea of financial stability as a reason *to* get married.[2]

There also appears to be a distinction on marriage when it comes to age. The survey found that in the 1960s nearly seven out of ten twenty-somethings were married. But in 2008 that number was dramatically different. Just 26 percent of those in that same category were married. Unlike their parents, this age group sees cohabitation in a much more favorable light than the generation before them.[3]

The Pew survey also examined the question of "What is a family?" More than 85 percent said a family is a "married couple, a married couple with children or a single parent with children." But 63 percent said gay couples with children are also a "family."[4]

One other very interesting and important component was a question on the survey dealing with premarital sex. In 1969, during the height of the sexual revolution, 68 percent said premarital sex is wrong. In 2009, only 32 percent said it is wrong.[5] As fewer and fewer people think sex before marriage is wrong, more and more people are getting sexually transmitted diseases (the Centers for Disease Control estimated that 19 million new infections occur each year[6]) and having unplanned pregnancies (71.5 per 1000 teenage girls in 2006[7]). Sadly, we can see that the shouting merchants of Vanity Fair seem to be having no trouble selling their "wares."

BAD IDEAS HAVE *BAD* CONSEQUENCES

Remember back in the early 1990s when Dan Quayle created a cultural firestorm by discussing the CBS TV character Murphy Brown? The situation comedy portrayed a TV anchorwoman, played by Candice Bergen, having a child out of wedlock. The former vice president gave a speech in San Francisco denouncing the idea, calling it part of a greater problem in America. He identified the issue as the "poverty of values," which included a greater acceptance of unwed motherhood and the absence of fathers. In the speech, he said: "It doesn't help matters when primetime TV has Murphy Brown, a character who supposedly epitomizes today's intelligent, highly paid professional woman, mocking the importance of fathers by bearing a child alone and calling it just another lifestyle choice."[8]

Time magazine wrote that Quayle deserved "points for audacity" for stepping into the controversy.[9] While numerous scathing editorials cropped up in newspapers all across the country, Barbara DeFoe Whitehead came to his defense in a piece that appeared in the *Atlantic Monthly*, entitled "Dan Quayle Was Right."[10]

In her article, Whitehead offered a plethora of evidence from social science that underscores some important truths about families and children: that single parent households are more often in poverty (six times as likely to be poor); two to three times more likely to have children with emotional or behavioral problems; and have children who are more susceptible to getting pregnant, using drugs, dropping out of school, or getting in trouble with the law.[11] This data should serve as a wake-up call for the Church to embrace our single-parent families and provide them with the support they so desperately need. Single parents are doing a job that God designed for two people—and it's tough enough when *both* Mom and Dad are doing the job!

Dan Quayle *was* right, but far more importantly, *God* is always right. He created families with mothers and fathers because each has an important job to play in the life of the child, and neither can ever fully do the other's job. Sex outside of marriage creates the potential for some pretty awful consequences, not just for ourselves but for our children as well. As wrong a decision as it is to have sex outside of marriage (with all of the bad consequences), what about divorce in this country? What is that doing to the heart of our nation, and what is it doing in the hearts of our children?

THE DIVORCE ROLLER COASTER

When it comes to divorce in this country, there is some good news and some bad news. First, the good news.

According to a report from the U.S. Census Bureau released in May of 2011, entitled "Number, Timing and Duration of Marriages and Divorces: 2009," the number of divorces in America is leveling off (that's the partial good news). This comes on the heels of decades of increase in the numbers of divorces.[12]

The information shows that women between the ages of 50 and 59 who had been married had a 41 percent divorce rate. That sounds high, but in 2004, that number was 44 percent.[13]

Here's something else the report says, and it is more *good* news, in an otherwise bad news story. Fifty-five percent of married couples have been married for at least fifteen years. And 35 percent have celebrated their twenty-fifth anniversaries. Six percent have hit the fifty-year mark. All of these numbers show a positive increase since 1996.[14]

For 72 percent of all couples, both husband and wife were in their first marriage. That's up about 3 percent points for both men and women since the 1980s. That's pretty good, considering the survey also found only 6 percent were wives in a second marriage and 8 percent were husbands in their second marriage as well. Another 8 percent found both spouses in their second marriage.[15]

But, the census report shows some disturbing trends as well. Groucho Marx had a unique way of looking at divorce. He said, "Marriage is the chief cause of divorce."[16] There's the humor. Now here's the bad news.

For those marriages that *do* end in divorce, the median life of the marriage is about eight years, according to the Census Bureau study. Those who did divorce and remarry did so within four years.[17] The report seems to indicate a few reasons why we are seeing a decline in the numbers of divorces (don't get your hopes up, the reason is *not* good). It appears that one of the main reasons is that there has been a jump in the number of couples cohabitating or living together without getting married. For biblically minded Christians, that can't be viewed as something positive.

Living together without getting married, or cohabitation, is on the rise. In the Pew Research survey, 44 percent of all adults (and more than half of all adults ages thirty to forty-nine) say they have cohabitated at some point in their adult life. And for those who have, 64 percent saw this as a step forward to marriage.[18]

Does living together provide an opportunity to "try out" commitment before actually committing? Was divorce from the 1970s and 1980s so prolific and so painful that it has given license to couples in the twenty-first century to try to avoid hurt by simply avoiding marriage? What does this mean for the future of marriage in this country?

The Census Bureau, based on data from 1996, had projected that one out of two first marriages would ultimately end in divorce; that's *one* out

***There is a* reason why God says He "hates divorce."** of *two*, up from one out of three a few decades earlier.[19] Some demographers are still predicting that despite the decline in divorces, we are still headed toward a 50 percent failure rate of first-time marriages. Mary Kay Blakely, author of *American Mom*, said that "Divorce is the psychological equivalent of a triple coronary bypass."[20] Anyone who has ever gone through one can agree. There is a reason why God says He "hates divorce" (Malachi 2:16 NKJV). He knows how much pain it causes His children—and He knows it leaves a broken and damaged heart.

But there seems to be one important word the report left out of all the social science date. L-O-V-E. Isn't that the key ingredient in any successful marriage? The Census Bureau didn't and can't define love, but God can and did. He wrote in His Word:

> Love is patient and kind; love does not envy or boast; it is not arrogant or rude. It is not easily angered. It does not insist on its own way; it is not irritable or resentful; it does not rejoice at wrongdoing, but rejoices with the truth. Love bears all things, believes all things, hopes all things, endures all things.
> (1 Corinthians 13:4–7 ESV)

Maybe that's what we need to keep marriages strong and vibrant: to really understand what *love* is by more clearly understanding who God is. C. S. Lewis described the interconnection between God and marriage with his typical eloquence when he said: "When I have learnt to love God better than my earthly dearest, I shall love my earthly dearest better than I do now."[21] There's the challenge as well as the answer.

The Pew Research Center survey asked one more, very important thing. The heart of the survey can be found in the question: "Is marriage obsolete?" For those between ages eighteen and forty-nine, four out of ten answered *yes*.[22] Now compare that information to the responses registered voters gave to *Time* magazine in 1978. More than thirty years ago, the

***Their faulty reasoning* has cohabitants thinking that somehow if the relationship ends, it will hurt less if the couple was never married.**

response was that 28 percent agreed that marriage was becoming obsolete.[23]

Yet, despite these alarming numbers, Americans remain upbeat about marriage and family. Sixty-seven percent say they are optimistic about the future of marriage in this country. That number is greater than those who are optimistic about our educational system (50 percent optimistic) and far more optimistic than our economic system (46 percent optimistic—and the survey was done in 2010, before the economy had gotten even worse).[24]

So how do we break down all this data and figure out what we are really hearing about marriage? First, divorce has clearly frightened people away from marriage. The age gap on the "obsolete" question is reflective of a generation who has felt and seen the impact of no-fault divorce. Not anxious to go through that kind of pain themselves, more and more couples are opting for "living in sin" as a way of working out the kinks of married life. Their faulty reasoning has cohabitants thinking that somehow if the relationship ends, it will hurt less if the couple was never married. Nothing could be further from the truth.

The couples who decide to cohabitate fail to take into consideration the data that also tells us that cohabitation is *not* a step forward to marriage but rather a step closer to divorce. Overwhelmingly, couples who live together before marriage are much more likely to see their marriages dissolved if they do get married.[25]

Jean Kerr may have been on to something when she noted that, "Being divorced is like being hit by a Mack truck. If you live through it, you start looking very carefully to the right and to the left."[26] The data from the Pew survey gives rise to the belief that there have been a whole lot of "traffic accidents" and if we are not very careful, there will be many more to come.

Marriage between a man and a woman was defined by God Himself. The question is not whether that model will become obsolete but rather whether we choose to live under the protective plan of God's design. Robert Anderson rightly notes that "in every marriage more than a week old, there are grounds for divorce. The trick is to find, and continue to find, grounds for marriage."[27]

MAKING THE IMPOSSIBLE POSSIBLE

When you think about the idea of marriage, it really doesn't make a whole lot of sense, from a mere mortal's perspective. Two people, one male and one female, make a promise (in front of witnesses) that they will love and cherish each other for a long time. How long? Until one of them dies!

They publicly pledge to each other all their worldly goods; they vow to stick together through thick and thin, richer or poorer, sickness and health. They seal their promise by giving each other rings to symbolize their eternal love and as a way of letting any other interested parties know that, from this day forward, they are no longer available. They are "off the market." Then they kiss, letting everyone in the room see that they, the new husband and the new wife, did this of their own free will and they did it out of *love*. What a picture of perfection. For one brief moment, time does stand still. We are transported back to that garden experience, that Eden, where sin had not yet arrived, where death was not yet a part of the earth, where man and woman could work in complete nakedness and know no shame. Perfection, just as God designed it.

Then sin showed up—and everything changed.

Today, sin is *still* here, and everything *has* changed, with the exception of one very important issue. God has not withdrawn His definition or His purpose for marriage. Man and woman, if they elect to marry, still step into the *mysterion*, the great mystery. Husband and wife still leave their parents' homes and become one flesh. God still instructs a wife to submit to her husband, and he, in return, is directed to love his wife while submitting to the Great Designer of marriage. All of this makes sense, at one level, if you envision marriage taking place in the perfect garden of Eden. But drop the concept of wedded bliss into a sin-sick, fallen world, and things quickly get out of focus. So, *why?* Why didn't God rewrite the instructions after sin came into the world?

Perhaps what God is showing us is the power of the mystery itself. Marriage becomes the tutorial for unconditional love. After the "I do's" we learn the language of, "I'm sorry," "I forgive you," and, "I want you." In marriage, we learn how the Gospel is manifested, through our obedience to God. Each day of our wedded life, we learn how to practice mercy, patience, self-control, and selflessness.

Each day of our wedded life, we learn how to practice mercy, patience, self-control, and selflessness.

We put into action the very attributes that define our Savior. We draw closer to Him, knowing that because of our sinful nature, we can't do any part of marriage on our own. We can't love, forgive, encourage, or affirm our mate effectively without Him. We come to realize that we need Him and we desperately want Him in our lives, our marriages and our homes.

Listen. Can you hear them? The merchants are shouting, *taunting,* some might say. They offer the cheap-trinket suggestion that "you never loved him anyway—get out of the relationship." Or they lure us closer to their wares by whispering, "She's growing fat. She's not the woman you married. You deserve someone younger, someone prettier." Or they put out on the sidewalk the cheapest goods of all, labeled with the words, "Just move in together. Work out the kinks first, and then make the lasting commitment. Go on. It'll work out just fine." Buy, buy *buy!* But buyer, *beware!*

Their goods are cheap and poorly made. They look shiny and bright on the outside, offering temporary excitement and moderate fulfillment. In truth, what the merchants are selling is nothing more than hollow ideas that will surely leave the "customer" empty and unsatisfied.

Vanity Fair is not an easy place to visit. Remember how Christian and Faithful were hesitant about entering the place before they understood that they "must needs pass through the town," as we must do. Don't hesitate. Let's boldly enter the marketplace, armed with the knowledge of God's Word, confident that the Creator of marriage Himself can give us all we need, through Him and by Him, to bring the Gospel into our marriages and experience the majesty of the *mystery*.

When we do, the merchants will stop shouting, recognizing the worthlessness of their own merchandise. Our marriages can and must be a witness to a world that longs to see Christianity in action—where "talk" and "walk" travel hand in hand. Let us show the world what *real* love, His love, looks like by role modeling it first in our own homes.

Will it be easy? Hardly! But it will be the experience of a lifetime.

I think Jack Benny, that great comedian, put in all into perspective when he said, "My wife Mary and I have been married for forty-seven years and not once have we had an argument serious enough to consider divorce; murder, yes, but divorce, never."

Making our marriages into what God Himself designed allows us a peek into the garden where we once lived, and where we will live with Him again someday.

The most merciful thing that a family does to
one of its infant members is to kill it.

Margaret Sanger[1]

Murder is once for all forbidden. Therefore, we may not
destroy even the fetus in the womb . . . To hinder a birth
is merely a speedier way to kill a human. It makes no
difference whether you take away a life that has been
born or destroy one that is not yet born.

Tertullian[2]

You made all the delicate, inner parts of
my bodyand knit me together in my mother's womb.
Thank you for making me so wonderfully complex!
Your workmanship is marvelous—how well I know it.
You watched me as I was being formed in utter
seclusion, as I was woven together in the dark of the
womb. You saw me before I was born. Every day of my
life was recorded in your book. Every moment was
laid out before a single day had passed.

King David, Psalm 139:13–16 NLT

10
The Cenote
of Sacrifice

Craig and I have been blessed with many opportunities to visit some interesting places around the globe. When we travel, we always make it a habit to look for evidence of God—His Truth, His message, and His people. We know deeply and very personally how real He is, but it is always so humbling and thrilling, when journeying across a big planet, to realize just how little we mortals are—and how majestic is our God. It is wonderful to be loved by a very big God, and we never have a problem finding His fingerprints. They are everywhere!

One year, we decided to take a trip to Cancun, Mexico, to find some rest along the world-famous, sandy beaches of the Yucatan peninsula. We thought we would put our beach towels down on the shoreline and simply warm ourselves for days like cats catching the last, warm rays of the afternoon sun. But given our personality types, our suntanning lasted a very limited time. In short order, we decided to do some exploring and look for *those* fingerprints.

We boarded a bus that took us to some fascinating Mayan ruins buried in the jungles of the peninsula. What we discovered was an ancient and advanced civilization. The Mayans had an unusual depth of understanding about mathematics and science. They even constructed a sophisticated astronomical observatory called El Caracol. In many respects, the Mayans were greatly ahead of their time; but in other ways, they were steeped in darkness and ignorance.

We climbed the stairs of the stone pyramid of Chichen Itza, flanked by the Feathered Serpents on either side of the El Castillo staircase. To the east of the pyramid is a building called the Temple of the Tables, so named for the series of altars located at the top of the structure. These altars are supported by carved masculine figures with upraised arms called "atlantes." On the altars, pagan priests would place their "sacrifices."

What caught our eye was a place not far from the main structures that was, for us, the very incarnation of evil. It is called the Cenote (Sacred Well) of Sacrifice.

The Cenote is a natural well of huge proportions that created a gaping hole in the floor of the jungle. It was hundreds of feet across and plunged down into a deep, dark pool of water below. Archeologists have mined the depths of this great shaft. What they found there is an ugly testimony to the fact that great cultural and scientific accomplishments of a society do not eradicate the reality of sin or moral depravity. At the bottom of the well, mired in the silt of the ages, lay the bones of children sacrificed to the pagan gods of the Mayans. The children were drugged, then wrapped with ropes and cloth before being weighted down with stones. Bound and dazed, the children were tossed into the well. The belief is that the children were murdered and their hearts removed (a common practice in the pagan Mayan culture) before they were thrown into the black abyss. The hearts of the victims would be placed on the altars of the great stone pyramid. The passing of thousands of years has silenced their screams.

MODERN-DAY ALTARS OF SACRIFICE

On January 22, 1973, the United States Supreme Court handed down what remains the most deadly decision ever to impact our country. *Roe v. Wade* (along with the companion decision, *Doe v. Bolton*, also decided in 1973) legalized abortion from the moment of conception up to the moment of birth. Fifty-three million children have lost their lives as a result.[3] The merchants in Vanity Fair have been most effective in wooing customers and selling their wares of death-on-demand.

The statistics swirling around this issue give proof to the fact that the marketing of death is apparently a very successful venture. Consider the following:

- Women in their twenties make up around half of all abortions.[4]
- Teenagers account for about 18% of all abortions.[5]
- 61% of abortions are accounted for by women who have had one child or more.[6]
- Half of the women seeking an abortion have already had at least one abortion.[7]
- 36% of abortions are performed on white women, 30% on black women, and 25% on Hispanic women.[8] (Note the disproportion, considering that approximately 73% of women in the U.S. are white, 13% are black and 16% are Hispanic.)[9]
- 37% of women getting abortions are Protestant; 28% are Catholic.[10]
- 18% of women who call themselves "born-again" Christians have had an abortion—that is nearly one out of five women who call themselves "born-again."[11]
- Nearly 43% of *all* women will have had an abortion by the time they are forty-five.[12]

The merchants of death are very successful, indeed. According to the National Right to Life Committee, Planned Parenthood, the nation's largest provider of abortions, had $902.8 million in total revenues during the 2005–2006 fiscal year. Thirty-eight percent, or $345.1 million of that came from "Health Center Income" or clinic revenues. Another 34 percent, or $305.1 million, came from "Government Grants and Contracts," coming out of the pockets of taxpayers via their federal, state, or local governments.[13] "At $162.3 million, 'Private Contributions and Bequests' accounted for only a quarter (24%) of the group's revenues. Income from

Many major newspapers prohibit use of the words "pro-life" and demand that the words "anti-abortion" be used instead. Shape the message and you win the debate.

the Guttmacher Institute, Planned Parenthood's special research affiliate, was at $7.2 million. 'Other Operating Revenue,' at $33 million, constitutes the remaining 4 percent."[14]

So how do the merchants get their message out—and do it *so* effectively?

Multiple studies have shown that those who work in the newsrooms of major media support (by overwhelming numbers) what is often referred to as "reproductive choice." In reporting the news, abortion rights advocates are quoted far more frequently than pro-lifers. Events, rallies, and political events that support abortion get much more coverage than do pro-life events. Editorial columns in our major newspapers promote "abortion rights" over the "right to life" by a margin of nearly 2 to 1.[15] I have had many reporters share with me privately that if their editors or supervisors knew they subscribed to pro-life values and it were made known, it could well cost them their jobs. Many major newspapers prohibit use of the words "pro-life" and demand that the words "anti-abortion" be used instead.[16] Shape the message and you win the debate.

Pro-abortion advocates dominate not only the national media but the entertainment industry as well. In 2011, ABC's *Grey's Anatomy*, a popular prime time medical drama, had several episodes where one of the main characters discussed wanting to get an abortion. She eventually got what she wanted and a viewing public was witness to a married, career woman not having to have her life "interrupted" by a pregnancy. It is no coincidence that this storyline appeared given the fact that the creator of *Grey's Anatomy* sits on the board of Planned Parenthood for Los Angeles.[17]

Another program, this time on NBC, portrayed a high school girl on *Friday Night Lights* wanting information on abortion. In the episode, the school principal happily supplied what the student was seeking, causing uproar in the community. Nevertheless, she went through with the abortion. A feminist blog site posted, when the story aired, that the writer was "rooting" for an abortion and hailed the program as a landmark for TV, not unlike Bea Arthur's *Maude*, who got an abortion the year before *Roe v. Wade* was handed down. She said the abortion was not only a "victory" for the TV character but for millions of women who "choose" abortion every year.[18]

Pro-abortion forces plan on more victories in the "court of public opinion." A new sitcom is in the works about an OB/GYN and the plans are to include abortions in the plotline.[19] The creator behind a vampire series on HBO, as well as the series *Six Feet Under* (which also included an abortion plot), has a new idea up his sleeve called "Wichita." This time, he wants to portray the life of the late and infamous late-term abortionist, George Tiller.[20] It is a pretty safe guess that the portrait of the abortionist will be positive—and the "anti-choice" folks will, of course, be demonized. Can't you hear the merchants shouting, "Buy, buy, *buy*"?

IGNORANCE IS NOT BLISS

Abortion is, stated plainly, a holocaust. Multiple millions of people (notice I didn't say "potential people," which is the language of those who support abortion-on-demand when referring to the unborn baby) have been silenced, never to be heard from. In numbers almost too big to comprehend, America has lost people *with* potential. Thousands and thousands of brokenhearted fathers and deeply wounded mothers have been left in the wake of this horrific juggernaut moving across our nation for the last several decades. But despite the staggering numbers, the influence of the media, and the power of politics, the follower of Jesus Christ cannot, *may not*, use ignorance as an excuse!

During another holocaust when more than six million Jews were

89

eradicated, citizens of the towns nearest the death camps are reported to have stated that they didn't know what was happening behind the barbed wire fences; they couldn't explain the clouds of black smoke pouring out over their villages on an ongoing basis. "We had no idea," was their excuse. But it wasn't just the townspeople.

During the historically significant trials at Nuremberg, Germany, the transcript of the trials shows how high up this "ignorance" excuse had climbed. The following is an excerpt from March 21, 1946, from the trial of Hermann Goering, who is being cross-examined by Sir David Maxell-Fyfe of the United Kingdom:

> Q. Let me remind you of the evidence that has been given before this Court, that as far as Auschwitz alone is concerned, 4,000,000 people were exterminated. Do you remember that?
>
> A. This I have heard as a statement here, but I consider it in no way proved—that figure I mean.
>
> Q. If you do not consider it proved, let me remind you of the affidavit of Hoettl, who was Deputy Group Leader of the Foreign Section, of the Security Section of Amt IV of the RSHA. He says that approximately 4,000,000 Jews have been killed in the concentration camps, while an additional 2,000,000 met death in other ways. Assume that these figures—one is a Russian figure, the other a German—assume they are even 50 per cent correct, assume it was 2,000,000 and 1,000,000, are you telling this Tribunal that a Minister with your power in the Reich could remain ignorant that that was going on?
>
> A. This I maintain, and the reason for this is that these things were kept secret from me. I might add that in my opinion not even the Fuehrer knew the extent of what was going on.[21]

Amazing, isn't it, that even the leaders of that hellish regime, built on death and destruction, claimed ignorance as their excuse? They did, and we *cannot*.

Will Rogers said something interesting about ignorance, for he understood its true danger. "When ignorance gets started, it knows no bounds," he said.

As believers, we are set free from ignorance. God's love and grace opens not only our hearts but our minds to see more clearly His Truth and how it applies to everything around us. There is no ambiguity in the Word of God that He and He alone is the author of *all* life. He determines when we shall be born, and likewise He knows when we end our pilgrim's progress here on earth.

Speaking of *Pilgrim's Progress*, John Bunyan, like Will Rogers, knew the dangers of ignorance. I am not sure if he ever studied Plato, but if he had, Bunyan would have discovered that Plato called ignorance the "root and stem of all evil." Bunyan understood for the believer, in particular, ignorance doesn't just make us stumble around in the dark—it leads down a path of destruction.

In Bunyan's classic, we read of the believer's encounter with ignorance. As Christian was approaching the Celestial City, he encounters a fellow by the name of—you guessed it—*Ignorance*. Christian questions this man's basis for what he believes about the path he is taking and his motivations for taking it. Ignorance's answers, which are based entirely on inward feelings of the heart, sound embarrassingly modern. In fact, listen to their conversation and ask yourself if this kind of faulty reasoning doesn't sometimes affect our Christian walk.

CHRISTIAN: *How is it, dear Ignorance, with your soul and God?*
IGNORANCE: *Very well, I hope, for I am always full of good thoughts that come into my mind and console me on the way.*
CHRISTIAN: *Will you share some of them with us? What have you been thinking?*
IGNORANCE: *Why, I think often of God and Heaven.*
CHRISTIAN: *So do all men.*
IGNORANCE: *But in my thoughts, I desire God and Heaven.*

CHRISTIAN: *So do many who may never see them. There is a sacred proverb that says, "The soul of the sluggard desireth, and hath nothing."*
IGNORANCE: *But I have given up all for them.*
CHRISTIAN: *One can think so and be mistaken. Giving up everything is much harder than many people imagine. What leads you to believe that you have given up all for God and Heaven?*
IGNORANCE: *My hearts tells me that I have.*
CHRISTIAN: *But is your heart reliable? The Bible says, "He that trusteth in his own heart is a fool."*
IGNORANCE: *That is spoken of a fool. I'm no fool. My heart is wise and good.*
CHRISTIAN: *But how do you know that? What means have you of testing your own heart?*
IGNORANCE: *My heart comforts me in the hope of Heaven.*
CHRISTIAN: *That may be through its deceitfulness. Jeremiah the prophet said, "The heart is deceitful about all things, and desperately wicked; who can know it?" A man's heart may give him hope when there are no grounds for his hope.*
IGNORANCE: *But my heart and life agree, so my hope is well grounded.*
CHRISTIAN: *What proof have you that your heart and life agree?*
IGNORANCE: *My hearts tells me so.*
CHRISTIAN: *Your heart tells you so! Except the Word of God bears witness, other testimony is of no value.*[22]

Can you hear the circular reasoning that Ignorance uses? Because he *felt* good ideas (according to *his* thinking anyway), the thoughts must be right—and therefore, they must be truth! He doesn't start with truth, he starts with his feelings, and then lets his feeling determine what is true.

Ignorance, like many of us at times, thinks that because he feels a certain way, it must be truth.

Did you find yourself thinking, "He makes a lot of sense. My life and heart *are* in agreement so I can't be mistaken"? Ignorance, like many of us at times, thinks that because he feels a certain way, it must be truth. This plays out so often on the issue of abortion. "I don't *feel* like having another baby right now, so abortion is okay." "I don't *feel* like having a pregnancy interrupt my career path, so abortion is a right option." "I don't *feel* like having to stand out at school with an unplanned pregnancy, so abortion is all right by me." Like Ignorance with his faulty reasoning, we can too often let feelings be interpreted as truth. But remember Christian's response, "The Word of God bears witness." Given our propensity to sin, our hearts can't be trusted. That is why God gave us His Word, His revealed Truth. It protects us, guides us, convicts us, and leads us in right directions.

The Bible speaks to this same issue: "There is a way that seems right to a man, but its end is the way to death" (Proverbs 14:12 ESV). God is the giver of life. He and He alone has the sovereign right to determine both its beginning and its end, not us and not our circumstances, regardless of our feelings.

THE WISDOM OF DR. SEUSS

The year was 1864, and the tide had turned. Abraham Lincoln, who staunchly opposed the expansion of slavery, won the presidential election. America had been bloodied and bowed over the question of whether or not the color of a man's skin determined if he was a person or if he was property. With Lincoln's election, our country was about to step out of the ugliest and bloodiest chapter of our history. Brother had fought against brother, neighbor against neighbor; and in the end, thousands had died.

The parallels between the slavery debate in the last half of the nineteenth century and the abortion debate today have often been noted. But it is crucial to point out the role Christians have played not only in the abolitionist movement but also in today's battle for life.

Consider the common elements between slavery and abortion. In the 1800s in America, slavery proponents had a powerful economic incentive to continue the trade. The Southern slave-holding states provided a full two-thirds of the world's cotton. They argued that the end of slavery would mean an end to much of the Southern states' financial base. In our age, the abortion industry tries to downplay the exploitative profits it has made at the expense of human life—but the profits are in the staggering billions of dollars.

Former abortionists have explained to me that they could make thousands of dollars a day just by doing abortions.

I have talked with many *former* abortion clinic directors who shared that abortions' costs are predicated on gestational age: The further along the pregnancy is, the more money it will cost for the abortion to be done. It is not at all uncommon to say to a woman on the procedure table that she must come up with more money for the procedure to be completed. Such a practice hardly seems *pro*-woman! Former abortionists have explained to me that they could make thousands of dollars a day just by doing abortions. It's not love, it's money that makes the world go 'round.

Note the legal parallel between slavery and abortion as well. The Dred Scott case involved a slave who had been taken to the state of Missouri (a slave state subject to the Missouri Compromise) to live with his slaveholder, but who had previously resided in free Illinois and the free territory of Wisconsin. But the US Supreme Court ruled that the slave had no rights as a "person" under the Fourteenth Amendment. Rather, the slave was "property" and had to be returned to the slaveholder from a slave state.

When the Court ruled in *Roe v. Wade,* it essentially did just what had been done years before in the *Scott v. Sanford* case—the court refused to acknowledge the personhood of the pre-born in *Roe* and ignoring the personhood of the slave in *Scott*. The horrific decision of 1973 continues to deny the status of human being to generations of little ones whose voices we will never hear.

The pro-life movement of today, like the abolitionist movement before it, is fueled by the fervor of committed Christians who are not acting on feelings but on facts from God's Word. In 1804, a judge in Chatham County, Georgia, warned a grand jury under his charge that the curse of slavery was the work of men, not of God. He urged the jury to consider gradual but eventual emancipation, civic education, and Christian instruction for every former slave.[23]

In 1830, a pamphlet was circulated, entitled *An Address to the People of North Carolina on the Evils of Slavery*. It declared slavery "contrary to the plain and simple maxims of Christian Revelation, or religion of Christ."[24] During the slavery debate in Virginia, Philip A. Bolling, a Piedmont area delegate to the state legislature, voiced the observation that "This, sir, is a Christian community. They read in their Bibles 'do unto all men as you would have them do unto you'—and this golden rule and slavery are hard to reconcile."[25]

Mary Blackford of Fredericksburg, Virginia, opposed slavery openly in 1832. She lived across the street from a slave trader. Upon learning that the trader was going to sell a young male slave, Blackford approached the man and demanded that the young boy be given permission to see his mother and say his final goodbyes before his departure. The slave trader was unmoved. Mary wrote later, "I fixed my eyes steadily upon the hard-hearted being before me and asked him if he did not fear the judgment of an offended God."[26] Mary ran a clandestine Sunday school for slaves, even though it was illegal to do so. Twice she was threatened by a grand jury for teaching the Bible to slave children. Yet, for the sake of the Cross, she would not stop.

Today the fight for life is being led by Christians who understand the same thing Christians knew to be true in the 1800s. People, all people, regardless of their skin color or their size, are made in the image of God. Human beings are not property to be disposed of simply because they are deemed to be inconvenient or unplanned. Pregnancy help centers in this country now number more than 4,000, outnumbering the abortion clinics in this nation.[27] I love to speak at the annual banquets for Pregnancy Help Centers and have done so from Hawaii to Florida. When I am with these dear brothers and sisters, I know I have been in the presence of heroes. These tender mercy-givers love women right where they are, walk them through their fears, give them sound medical information, and offer them the option of learning to raise their baby or putting their baby in the arms of a couple who long for a child of their own. But the most important and most powerful component of these CPCs is the love of Christ they show through the work they do. Thousands of women have come to know the Lord as their personal Savior because of the compassionate kindness of someone at one of the centers. At pregnancy help centers, lives are saved not just temporally but eternally.

Dr. Seuss, the beloved author of children's books like *Green Eggs and Ham* and *The Cat in the Hat*, had a marvelous way of distilling big ideas into small but powerful thoughts. One of his characters once said, "Sometimes the questions are complicated and the answers are simple."[28] He illustrated that truism when he wrote *Horton Hears a Who*. In his creative story of friendship, Dr. Seuss (Theodor Geisel) introduces us to Horton, a lumpy and lovable elephant who is loyal to his friends. In the tale, Horton makes a declaration that resonates with Truth. While not citing Scripture, this unforgettable character nonetheless summarizes God's Truth by saying, "A person's a person, no matter how small."[29]

That's how God sees us—fearfully and wonderfully made—knit together, right under our mother's beating heart. Each of us is a person to God—no matter our size. He knows us intimately—even before we breathe our first breath outside of Mama. That is a fact Mr. Ignorance cannot ignore.

The truth is incontrovertible. Malice may attack it,
ignorance may deride it, but in the end, there it is.
Winston Churchill[30]

Abortion is either OK or it's not.

Peggy Noonan[1]

We must stop this love affair with the fetus.

Joycelyn Elders[2]

Shall the throne of iniquity, which
devises evil by law, have fellowship
with You? They gather together
against the life of the righteous,
and condemn innocent blood.

Psalm 94:20–21 NKJV

11
Nothing New under the Sun

The writer of Ecclesiastes really was right when he put down the words, "There is nothing new under the sun" (Ecclesiastes 1:9 NIV). Satan has been prowling around, attempting to take the lives of children almost since human beings walked out of the garden. Satan hates the miracle of life because it gives evidence to the existence of God. Satan can't give life; only God can. We were not made in the image of the "father of lies," but we are molded to look like Him who made us. God gives life—and the Devil traffics in death.

We don't have to look much further than Exodus's first chapter to find abortion being used by the Chief Liar himself. A proud, pompous earthly king couldn't stand the Hebrews. They bred like rabbits, he thought. They must be stopped or he, great Pharaoh of Egypt, would lose both his crown and his authority. Something had to be done. So he gave a directive to the Hebrew midwives: "When you serve as midwife to the Hebrew women and see them on the birthstool, if it is a son, you shall kill him but if it is a daughter, she shall live" (Exodus 1:16 ESV). The Hebrew word for the "birthstool" is *obnayim*, which means literally "two stones." The Hebrew mama would sit on the two stones and, with the help of gravity and the midwife, deliver her baby. Just think, ladies, no epidural—*yikes!*

But what is significant is that Satan, through Pharaoh, was trying to kill a child before he even took his first breath—the very definition of an abortion. In fact, to be more accurate, the description found in Exodus chapter 1 sounds eerily like a partial-birth abortion, one of the most barbaric forms of abortion today.

Two of the Hebrew midwives are named in the Bible, which is significant (Exodus 1:15). If you were going to be named in Scripture, you would probably want to be remembered for having done something *right* rather than for having done something *wrong*. In the case of these midwives, they did something *very* right. They disobeyed Pharaoh and trusted God—not too shabby when you realize these women were slaves and the consequences of their disobedience might have been very grave. Shiphrah and Puah (yes, those are their names) offered the kind of stellar argument that would make any defense attorney proud. They told Pharaoh that those Hebrew women were just easy "birthers"—babies came fast, much faster than Egyptian women's babies came. "So, sorry, Pharaoh, but it was too late by the time we got there." Case closed. The verdict? God blessed the midwives with children of their own, and the Bible says the Hebrews multiplied—which was just the opposite of what Pharaoh and Satan were trying to achieve (Exodus 1:20).

When Pharaoh was unable to get the Hebrew midwives to do what he wanted, he sent out what would be known today as an Executive Order. He commanded all his people to throw every baby boy born into the river but to let the little girls live. But one very faithful Hebrew mother, like those courageous midwives, trusted God when she gave birth to a little boy who would change history forever. Under the influence of Satan, abortion and infanticide were being practiced in ancient Egypt, just as they are being practiced today. There really is *nothing* new under the sun.

PAGAN PRACTICES

Thumb past a few more Old Testament books, and go to 1 Kings 18. Here we read the amazing story of the prophet Elijah taking on the prophets of Baal on top of windy Mount Carmel. Craig and I have stood on the spot many times, and it never ceases to amaze us that right there God had so clearly shown His power and His might to a people who were "limping" between two opinions about God. As you stand looking down into the valley of Megiddo, your heart begins to race, knowing that history will again take place in that same place. Someday our King Eternal will ride into a fierce battle, the most horrific conflict the world has ever seen, and victory will once again be His.

Evil King Ahab and his nasty wife Jezebel (now there's a marriage made in hell) were proud pagan worshipers. Their favorite deities were Baal and Asherah, a kind of husband and wife pagan deity couple. Ahab and Jezebel couldn't tolerate the prophet Elijah for lots of reasons. First, Elijah was messing with the economy. Elijah told Ahab there would be "no rain for three years." In the East, no rainfall means famine, which means economic collapse. Bad news if you are a king.

Second, this royal yet morally bankrupt couple were in the business of butchering the prophets of the Lord—of which Elijah *was* one! The message and the methods of Elijah were, to them, totally unacceptable. He must be killed. But God had other plans. When Elijah and Ahab met face-to-face, the prophet offered a challenge: "You bring your 450 prophets of Baal and your 400 prophets of Asherah," he told Ahab, "and let's meet over there—on that mountain. Your pagan priests will know where it is. They always like to build altars on high places."

Eight hundred and fifty pagan priests showed up, ready to do theological battle. They are fully convinced their despicable deities will manifest their powers on that high place and show the troublesome prophet of the Lord once and for all who is God—make that *god*, with a small *g*. To quote a line out of the movie *Secretariat*, directed by the brilliantly gifted writer and fellow Christian Randy Wallace, the priests of darkness were, "'bout to see something they ain't never seen before!"

Elijah then offered a challenge—simple and direct. The bad guys (those would be the pagans) and the good guy (that would be Elijah) would each build an altar, slaughter a bull, cut the animal into pieces, lay it on the wood, but not add fire. (Elijah was setting the stage for something *very* spectacular!) Once the altars were constructed, they would each call on the name of their gods. The god who answers, Elijah explains, "He is God" (1 Kings 18:24 ESV).

The pagan priests called out to their god to respond to the challenge put forth by Elijah. The *real* god, either Baal or Yahweh, would answer by fire, burning up what was on the sacrificial altar. It must have been a very curious sight to see these strange priests of darkness calling out to a god who is not there. The Bible tells us they shouted and shouted and shouted—from morning until nighttime. They shouted so long and so loud, that Elijah just couldn't help himself. He had to point out the obvious: NO ONE WAS THERE.

God is letting Ahab know, in no uncertain terms, that this Baal, this pagan god, is a pipsqueak, dinky deity.

You don't read sarcasm very often in Scripture, but it is clearly evident in 1 Kings 18:27. Elijah told the pagans to shout even louder and then proffered the idea that perhaps their god is, using the words of our British friends, "in the loo" (the bathroom). The pagan prophets of Baal responded by shouting even louder and cutting themselves with their own swords, until they had covered themselves with blood.

You *know* Who *did* show up! With a mighty display of His majesty and power, the One True God ignited, with the fire of heaven, not only the thrice-soaked altar of Elijah, but He incinerated the bull, the wood, the stones, and the dust! Any questions? The Lord, HE is God! It turned out to be a very bad day for the evil prophets. Elijah ordered them to be captured and killed.

So how does the story of God's power displayed on Mount Carmel tie into the issue of abortion? Glad you asked.

Bible archeology is a fascinating science. We learn so much when the stones cry out—and the stones have a lot to say! Ancient history tells us that Baal was considered the god over the weather. The myth tells us that he was the one who could make it rain and fertilize the fields. It was no accident (nothing is *ever* an accident with God) that Elijah let the evil king know in chapter 17 of 1 Kings that a drought is coming. The prophet's message was the equivalent of the European slap across the face with a glove—step one in any duel. God is letting Ahab know, in no uncertain terms, that this Baal, this pagan god, is a pipsqueak, dinky deity. "Take that, Ahab, no rain!" No wonder Ahab is bent on tracking down the prophet and killing him.

In the temples of Baal and Asherah, male and female prostitutes would engage in sexual acts with pagan worshipers in order to cause the god Baal to fertilize Asherah, often considered Mother Earth. You get the idea—sexual immorality was paramount and, according to the pagans, *necessary*. But it gets much darker the more we dig, literally.

Baal worship involved the killing of children. Another prophet, this time a weeping one, described how the high places were built to Baal to make a place where worshipers would sacrifice their sons on an altar of fire (Jeremiah 19:5). We read later in the same book that high altars were constructed, where both sons and daughters "passed through the fire." Death became a form of worship (Jeremiah 32:35). But the killing of children didn't end there.

We often ignore a crucial part of the Christmas story that doesn't fit well into Christmas carols or joyous pageants.

In Carthage, the particularly pagan capital of the Phoenician Empire, child sacrifice was commonplace. Archeologists have discovered stone altars on which children were sacrificed, and stone markers have been found that note the burial places of the remains. On the stones are markings that clearly indicate child sacrifice was a regular occurrence. Small earthen jars have also been dug up and found to contain the skeletal remains of children who were slaughtered. As if all of these discoveries weren't enough, entire burial grounds containing the remains of sacrificed children have also been discovered. Satan has been in the business of slaughtering children for a long, long time. *Roe v. Wade* is just the American version what he has been doing for centuries.

THE GREAT KILLER

We often ignore a crucial part of the Christmas story that doesn't fit well into Christmas carols or joyous pageants. In truth, there is nothing merry about this part of the story, but it is, nevertheless, a part of the Christmas message that cannot be ignored.

In the book of Matthew, chapter 2, we read that Jesus was born in Bethlehem during the reign of Herod the Great. The king earned that title because he was always building—palaces, fortresses, and even the temple in Jerusalem. But greatness is not a term that can be used to describe the way he led his people. In that way, Herod was anything but great.

Word came into Herod's throne room that wise men from the East were following a star that would lead them to the One said to be the King of the Jews. The magi wanted to worship this newborn King. A message like that doesn't sit well with an earthly king, particularly when he believed his own kingdom was being threatened. Herod instructed the wise men to find the Child and bring back word to inform the "Great" one exactly where the baby was. The star led the wise men to a house where they fell to their knees and worshiped the true Great One and offered Him gifts.

God protected these magi who wisely recognized and worshiped this Baby for who He *really* was. He used a dream to warn the magi that Herod was seething because he hadn't received what he commanded them to deliver. So the magi traveled back to their homes by another way, avoiding Herod altogether. When word reached the king that the wise men had refused to report back the location of the baby, his rage and wrath took the form of a deadly edict. Herod demanded that all baby boys, aged two and under, be killed. Children were butchered because they inconveniently stood in the way of the plans of the Great one. Herod exercised the right to choose. He practiced his "freedom of choice," and he *chose* to kill countless numbers of little boys. He was king and he had that right, or so he thought. After all, killing was nothing new to Herod. He had ordered the deaths of three of his own grown children.

The prophet Jeremiah is a part of this story as well. He had foretold of the horrific, barbaric act when he proclaimed: "A voice was heard in Ramah, weeping and loud lamentation, Rachel weeping for her children; she refused to be comforted because they are no more" (Matthew 2:18 ESV).

How many women today can't be comforted because their children are "no more"? How many lives have been damaged because the Great Deceiver has rattled his tail and whispered that a child can easily interrupt your plans and be disposed of more easily still? Pharaoh, pagan priests, and Herod—all were in the business of death-on-demand: They demanded it, and children died. Today the government allows abortion, and children *still* die.

Perhaps no issue in our culture elicits such emotion as abortion. The controversy has alienated friends, divided churches, and devastated individuals. Why? Because abortion is about people—*people,* made in the image of God, who have perished. It is also about *people* responsible for advancing this doctrine of death—and about *people* who have remained silent while abortion roars all around them. But abortion is also about *people* who have stood fast for God's Truth in the midst of an opposing culture.

Fifty-three million people have lost their lives since abortion was made legal in this country. The merchants have been selling and customers have been buying a most deadly concept. As you and I walk through this busy marketplace of ideas, we have to ask ourselves the same question over and over again: "Is Truth absolute?" Is there some transcendent moral code, bigger than any of us, that applies to *all* people, in *all* times, and in *all* circumstances? Or do we let our circumstances define what Truth is, for the moment? Does each of us decide individually what Truth is?

If we let our circumstances define what is our "temporary Truth," if our ever-changing situation creates our ethics, then we are more or less making up what is right and wrong as we go along. What is true one day might not be true the next. What is true for one person is probably not true for another. In the end, we will each do "what is right in [our] own eyes" (Judges 17:6 ESV).

Conversely, if we believe there is a divinely drafted code of morality—absolute Truth that wraps itself around whatever circumstance in which we find ourselves—we discover not only real freedom but complete protection. If abortion is wrong because God is the giver of all life, *and* if each human being is made in the image of God, *and* if the circumstances of one's conception should not determine whether or not an individual has a right to live, then we are left with only one choice—*life!*

Government, the secular media, and the entertainment industry may have made an unholy alliance with the merchants of death, but we, the Pilgrims who pass through this bustling market, do not need to buy their wares. What they are selling is an ancient idea. We too, like Christian and Faithful, can respond that we only "buy the Truth"—something much older than the merchants' lies and something that will last for all eternity.

But may I also suggest that, while we travel through Vanity Fair, we also take the time to lovingly share the Truth with those wounded, frightened "shoppers" in crisis who stand before the Great Deceiver, ready to "purchase" his goods? Let us remind them that there is a better, gentler, and more loving path they can follow, a different path that, like the magi, will lead them safely home.

Careless seems the great Avenger; history's pages but record
One death-grapple in the darkness 'twixt old systems and the
Word; Truth forever on the scaffold, Wrong forever on the throne—
Yet that scaffold sways the future, and, behind the dim unknown,
Standeth God within the shadow, keeping watch above His own.
James Russell Lowell[3]

In itself, homosexuality is as limiting as
heterosexuality: the ideal should be to be
capable of loving a woman or a man;
either, a human being, without feeling
fear, restraint, or obligation.

Simone de Beauvoir[1]

"Gay marriage" will inevitably undermine all marriages.

Chuck Colson[2]

Husbands, love your wives, as Christ loved the church
and gave himself up for her . . . husbands should
love their wives as their own bodies. He who loves his
wife loves himself. For no one ever hated his own flesh,
but nourishes and cherishes it, just as Christ does the
church, because we are members of his body.
"Therefore a man shall leave his father and mother and
hold fast to his wife, and the two shall become one flesh.

Paul, letter to the Ephesians, 5:25, 28–31 ESV

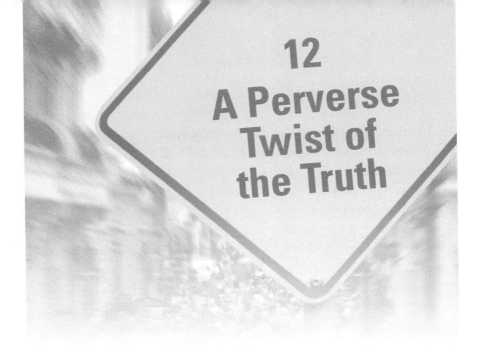

12

A Perverse Twist of the Truth

In today's marketplace of ideas, one of the most contentious issues is the topic of homosexuality. From TV talk shows to prime-time sitcoms and major motion pictures, America is being indoctrinated on the subject of homosexuality. The goal of those doing the indoctrinating is to garner full acceptance from all corners of society for not only homosexuality but lesbianism, bisexuality, and transgenderism. Look around, and it will become obvious to you that the so-called gay rights movement *appears* to be succeeding.

I remember flying back into Washington, DC in 1993 after giving a speech out of town. As the plane tipped it wings toward Ronald Reagan National Airport, I spotted a huge crowd marching down Constitution Avenue. Tens of thousands of people had come to the nation's capital to march for what they called same-sex rights and liberation.

The organizers passed out flyers to attendees, declaring their demands and their platform for change. In part, the flyer stated the following:

> We demand passage of a Lesbian, Gay, Bisexual, and Transgender civil rights bill and an end to discrimination by state and federal governments including the military; repeal of all sodomy laws and other laws that criminalize private sexual expression between consenting adults.

We demand legislation to prevent discrimination against Lesbians, Gays, Bisexuals and Transgendered people in the areas of family diversity, custody, adoption and foster care and that the definition of family includes the full diversity of all family structures.

We demand full and equal inclusion of Lesbians, Gays, Bisexuals and Transgendered people in the educational system, and inclusion of Lesbian, Gay, Bisexual and Transgender studies in multicultural curricula.

We demand the right to reproductive freedom and choice, to control our own bodies, and an end to sexist discrimination.

We demand an end to discrimination and violent oppression based on actual or perceived sexual orientation, identification, race, religion, identity, sex and gender expression, disability, age, class, AIDS/HIV infection.[3]

That event wasn't the first such march on Washington. There were similar protests going back to 1979 and as recently as 2009. Each time, speakers have demanded that proposals be made through legislation and that homosexuality not only be universally accepted, but laws changed to further facilitate the lifestyle.

Go back and read the list of demands again, and you can't help noticing the indoctrinators have achieved just about everything on their 1993 wish list. But notice something else, something extremely significant in that last demand. The change-agents demanded an end to discrimination or "oppression" based on . . . *religion.* Now this is where the debate gets very interesting.

FAULTY INTERPRETATIONS FOR SINFUL SUPPORT

Perhaps the most egregious aspect of the whole "gay rights" debate is the way the unblemished Word of God is twisted and turned like a pretzel at the state fair by those who seek to use it as a silencing tool. This so-called Gay Gospel is a humanist creation that goes to the heart of that

110

demand to stop "religious oppression." It's really a very clever approach: Take the Scriptures, stand them on their head, and then use it *against* those who actually believe what the Bible has to say and take its meaning as Truth.

Consider this example. Retired Episcopal bishop John Shelby Spong has long been considered a leading spokesman for progressive Christianity. Loosely translated, "progressive Christianity" means taking a sort of "pick and choose" approach to the Bible, keeping the parts one likes and disposing of those that are personally uncomfortable or deemed to be no longer relevant to modern society. It also means abandoning the concept that the Word of God is, in fact, God-breathed and inspired. Progressives embrace the idea that several human authors wrote some interesting ideas but those ideas are not necessary transcendent Truth.

In 2005, Spong wrote a book entitled *The Sins of Scripture*. In his work, he posits the idea that homosexuality is actually imposed by God on people who fail to worship Him properly. He alleges that the apostle Paul believed that homosexuality was, in fact, a punishment for sin. Spong also writes that Paul was a "religious fanatic." But he goes one step further by declaring that fanatics are usually people suppressing something so unacceptable deep within themselves that they can't admit it to themselves.[4] In other words, he's saying that Paul was gay! Yes, there are some very strange ideas being sold in Vanity Fair!

Another common abuse of Scripture used to promote homosexuality is the idea that the real sin of the twin cities of Sodom and Gomorrah was not sexual immorality but rather the problem of being inhospitable. So where does that idea come from?

An ancient Canaanite custom was the guarantee of protection for guests who came into a home. In Genesis 19:8, Lot says "Don't do anything to these men, for they have come under the protection of my roof" (NIV). These *men* are, in fact, angels. Lot then offers his own daughters to the angry mob to appease their sexual appetites. That act alone shows what living in a reprobate culture like Sodom's can do to the human spirit. This father knows his daughters are virgins, and yet he is willing to sacrifice their innocence. He says that they have "known" no man. That word *known* doesn't mean "got acquainted"—it means having had sexual intercourse. In offering his *own* daughters, Lot violates his *own* directive to the crowd not to act "wickedly." Offering your children to be raped by a mob is nothing short of wicked.

Yet gay activists take this event in history and stand the facts on their head by proffering the idea that Lot was inhospitable to the crowd by keeping them out while keeping the angels in. His guests weren't "known" to the mob, so Lot must have been behaving in an inhospitable manner. To say that this is a stretch would be a grand understatement.

Over and over again, "gay" theologians will spout that Jesus said nothing about homosexuality so therefore it must not be an issue and it must not be wrong. An argument from silence is no argument at all. Jesus did not teach about prostitution, rape, incest, or bestiality, but that doesn't mean that He wasn't opposed to any of them or that He approved of all of them.

Jesus clearly affirms the model of marriage—one man and one woman—in the New Testament (Matthew 19:5). The upholding of the Genesis model by Jesus supports the claim that the Bible maintains a continuum that marriage is inarguably between a man and a woman. The Scripture also clearly articulates that sexual expression is not only permissible but encouraged only within the confines of that relationship. Telling generations to "rejoice in the wife of your youth" (Proverbs 5:18 NIV) and that the marriage bed is undefiled (Hebrews 13:4) are crystal clear declarations of what marriage is and where sex belongs.

RIGHT WORD, RIGHT WAY

The Church of Jesus Christ and those who love His Word are the solution to this modern deception. Rather than listening to the siren's song of the gay theologians that lures both nonbelievers and believers crashing into the rocks of wrongful thinking, the men and women who know and love Jesus can redirect this debate with sound doctrine and grace-filled words.

Homosexuality was rampant in first-century Rome. Paul knew how saturated in sin the culture was. He has barely begun his letter to the church in Rome when he denounces same-sex behavior. But again, the proponents of homosexuality have tried to reduce the meaning of Romans 1:26–27 to signify that Paul was really addressing homosexual promiscuity, as if to say that being "faithful and monogamous" as a homosexual was permissible. Is that what Paul was saying? That argument may play well in the secular press and on some college campuses but the apostle was not an ignorant man.

He lived in a world where the Greeks glorified "love" between a man and a boy. When Craig and I visited the ruins at Pompeii, we saw the obscene graffiti on the walls of the brothels left standing after the eruption of Mount Vesuvius. Paul would have seen that same kind of graffiti in Rome. He knew that the emperors of the day were steeped in sexual debauchery. Orgies were commonplace, and the Greek ideal of same-sex relationships was the only excuse needed for the most base of

From the opening **chapters of Genesis to the return of the Bridegroom for His bride in Revelation, the definition and model of marriage is one man and one woman.**

behaviors. Paul saw, with absolute clarity, that Rome had "exchanged the truth about God for a lie" (Romans 1:25 ESV). Sadly, we are witnessing the very same manifestation today.

The strongest argument for the Church—and for those of us who have ventured into Vanity Fair desiring to declare Truth—is not the argument *against* homosexuality but rather it is the argument *for* monogamous heterosexual marriage.

Leviticus 18:22 and 20:13 condemn the act of men "lying" with men but we cannot overlook passages like those found in Deuteronomy 5:18, where the fiery pen of God etches into stone the commandment to "not commit adultery."

God makes His Truth wonderfully clear if we allow His Spirit to be our teacher. From the opening chapters of Genesis to the return of the Bridegroom for His bride in Revelation, the definition and model of marriage is one man and one woman. Scripture tells us repeatedly that sexual expression is relegated to that relationship and nowhere else. There is no ambiguity on God's position on this topic!

God not only created sex (now that's a stunner for those who think this was an idea that came from MTV), but He lovingly made us sexual beings. Sex is not wrong or sinful. But where sexual behavior is expressed becomes the flashpoint. The merchants of the marketplace, like Simone de Beauvoir, want us to believe that sexual expression should be without "fear, restraint, or obligation." God, on the other hand, has clearly directed otherwise. Love wildly, deeply, passionately, madly—but let your husband or wife be the only focus of your passion.

> *Can we truly* afford to "exchange the truth for lie" and not think that there will be horrific consequences?

C. S. Lewis described this perfectly when he said, "The monstrosity of sexual intercourse outside marriage is that those who indulge in it are trying to isolate one kind of union (the sexual) from all the other kinds of union which were intended to go along with it and make up the total union."[5]

This entire debate can be distilled into two words: "biblical authority." Either we take the Word of God to mean what it says and recognize it for the transcendent Truth that it is, or we abandon ourselves to the idea that we alone are the final arbiters of truth. Can we truly afford to "exchange the truth for lie" and not think that there will be horrific consequences?

Jeremy Taylor, the great English clergymen of the 1600s, once said, "Marriage is the mother of the world. It preserves kingdoms, and fills cities and churches, and heaven itself."[6] We only need look around and see the Truth of God's Word in action to know that he was right.

Under patriarchy, no woman is safe to live her life, or to love, or to mother children. Under patriarchy, every woman is a victim, past, present, and future. Under patriarchy, every woman's daughter is a victim, past, present, and future. Under patriarchy, every woman's son is her potential betrayer and also the inevitable rapist or exploiter of another woman.

Andrea Dworkin[1]

I didn't marry you because you were perfect. I didn't even marry you because I loved you. I married you because you gave me a promise. That promise made up for your faults. And the promise I gave you made up for mine. Two imperfect people got married and it was the promise that made the marriage. And when our children were growing up, it wasn't a house that protected them; and it wasn't our love that protected them—it was that promise.

Thornton Wilder[2]

But from the beginning of creation, "God made them male and female." Therefore a man shall leave his father and mother and hold fast to his wife, and the two shall become one flesh. So they are no longer two but one flesh. What therefore God has joined together, let not man separate.

Mark 10:6–9 ESV

13
A Marriage Made in Heaven

Fellow Pilgrim, if you are reading this, then I have some news for you: You and I are *still* in captivity! As we travel through this life, we can take great comfort in knowing that each step takes us a tiny bit closer to our real home in glory. But until that day, when we stand (or fall to our knees) in the magnificence of His presence, we need only look around us to see that we are still exiled in a very sin-sick fallen world, in desperate need of the Savior. An ancient, weeping prophet knew that dichotomy very well.

Jeremiah had warned God's people not to abandon their love for Him. He knew the sins of their fathers would creep back into their lives and pagan worship would once again dominate their world, and when it did, captivity would be inevitable.

In 597 BC, tens of thousands of Jeremiah's countrymen were deported out of the land of milk and honey to a world filled with massive ziggurats adorned with statues of winged bulls. To comfort the captives in their exile, Jeremiah wrote them a letter. Let me remind you what he said regarding marriage and families: "Take wives and have sons and daughters; take wives for your sons, and give your daughters in marriage, that they may bear sons and daughters; multiply there, and do not decrease" (Jeremiah 29:6 ESV).

At first read, it seems like a rather strange request. The people of God were being held captive in a foreign place, far from all they had known or loved. The food tasted strange, the customs were different, and the clothes were unusual. No matter how the exiles looked at their surroundings, it wasn't home. Yet, in the midst of all that was neither familiar nor resembled anything from back home, the prophet Jeremiah directs them, through a letter, to have weddings and to get pregnant! Why?

Directing the Israelites to marry and have children—and then telling them that their children should *also* marry and have children—is a strong indication that the captives were going to be captives for a long, *long* time. But God is always perfect, and He is always purposeful!

God wanted His children to know that marriage is a great stabilizing factor for a society. The captives were to seek Babylon's peace. Creating families was a wonderful way of investing in the future of that foreign land; it would be good not only for the *captives* but for their *captors* as well.

So, fellow captive, what are the benefits of marriage as defined and designed by God Himself? Why would marriage be good not only for the Israelites but also for the Babylonians? Why is marriage, biblically defined, still good for us today?

According to the Heritage Foundation, a prestigious think-tank in Washington, DC, social science has shown through measurable metrics that marriage has multiple benefits. Consider the following:

Married women have higher levels of physical and psychological health.
Being married increases the possibility of financial affluence.
Married people have fewer problems with alcohol and depression.
Married men make more money.
Married women are less likely to experience poverty.
Married people live longer.[3]

In a letter from John Adams to Thomas Jefferson, dated July 16, 1814, Adams wrote, "As long as Property exists, it will accumulate in Individuals and Families. According to the evidence, as long as Marriage exists, Knowledge, Property and Influence will accumulate in Families!"[4]

Marriage has always been the cornerstone institution on which society rests. Thomas DeWitt Talmage was considered one of the greatest religious leaders in American in the mid- to late-nineteenth century. He knew the pivotal contributions of marriage and family. He wrote, "A church within a church, a republic within a republic, a world within a world, is spelled in four letters, H-O-M-E. If things go right there, they go right everywhere. The doorsill of the dwelling house is the foundation of the Church and the State."[5]

Marriage is good for society. But there is another reason for Jeremiah's assignment. The prophet understood that in a family, sons and daughters learn to honor their parents (Deuteronomy 5:16). This principle is so crucial that God etched it in stone with a pen of fire along with nine other commandments. When a legacy of faith is intentionally instilled in the home, children learn to love and obey God. In turn, that same legacy is then passed on from one generation to the next. Timothy knew the power of a praying grandmother in Eunice and of a godly mother in Lois. Two women, family members, helped mold a young man of God who would be used to carry on the work of Paul, and eventually he would help to change the world!

THE PRICE OF PERVERSION

Marriage was not only good for the Israelites in helping to protect the welfare of Babylon but marriage is equally as protective for our culture today. Conversely, sexual experimentation hurts not only a marriage but damages a nation as well.

In the letter to the Hebrews, we read that "marriage (is to) be held in honor among all" (Hebrews 13:4 ESV). God's principle is very clear: Marriage is one man, one woman. Radical redefinitions are prohibited by what we read in the very next line, "and let the marriage bed be undefiled, for God will judge the sexually immoral and adulterous" (Hebrews 13:4 ESV). Sexual immorality and adultery are clearly defined in Scripture as any sexual relationship outside of the bonds of marriage. Again, marriage has been defined as one man and one woman. So-called same-sex marriage is never permitted biblically. It defiles and dishonors marriage, as does adultery and sexual promiscuity.

For this Pilgrim, when I walk through Vanity Fair, I get the distinct impression that the merchants at the booth called "homosexuality" seem to be "shouting" the loudest. In part, they shout because they wish to silence those who will not "buy" their goods. Political correctness is a hot commodity in the marketplace today. Being "PC" has become a new, transcendent value that some say trumps biblical Truth—and far too many people are buying into the idea.

Political correctness is the concept that in order to conform (and be accepted), we must not only think but also express our beliefs in accordance with what is popular but not necessarily biblically correct. If we break this unwritten code, we are punished.

I have done scores of interviews with people who have paid a hefty price for not buying this shabby trinket, and I never cease to be amazed at the level of aggression by those who insist (like the merchants in Vanity Fair) that we become consumers of their worldview. Here are just a few examples:

- A Christian couple in England refused to rent rooms in their "bed and breakfast" to any couple that was not married, whether they were heterosexual or homosexual. They were sued and lost.[6]
- A woman was fired from a major department store for refusing to allow a "transgendered" man from using the women's dressing room.[7]
- A Christian couple was prohibited from continuing their work in foster care when they told a social worker that they would not tell children that homosexuality was an "acceptable" lifestyle.[8]
- A street preacher was arrested and held in a jail cell for telling a passerby that homosexuality was a sin in the eyes of God.[9]
- A fifteen-year-old wrote an opinion piece in his high school newspaper against gay adoption and was accused of breaking the schools "bullying" policy.[10]

Political correctness, like everything else that challenges the Church today, is not a new phenomenon. John Bunyan wrote that Christian and his new companion, Hopeful, encountered this issue shortly after leaving Vanity Fair. They met a man by the name of Mr. By-ends who declares that he is from the town of Fair-speech. He tells the travelers that he must "keep up with the times."[11]

But Christian challenges the man, whom Bunyan describes as wearing a "red velvet coat, having a dignified manner and an expansive waistline indicating that he was no beggar." In other words, Mr. By-ends is comfortably satisfied with himself and had no desire to "rock the boat." After all, he had to keep up with the times.

But Christian challenged this new acquaintance by telling him sternly that if they are to travel together, Mr. By-ends must "go against wind and tide. You must also own religion in his rags, as well as when in his silver slippers—and stand by him, too, when bound in irons, as well as when he walks the streets with applause."[12] What a fabulous word picture of what it means to stand *on* and *for* Truth! Bunyan is telling the reader that following Christ means that the Truth will sometimes be welcomed and received (wearing silver slippers) and sometimes it will be wholly rejected (wearing rags), but it remains the Truth nonetheless. Bunyan has more than sufficient gravitas for making this point; he penned those words sitting in a prison cell for preaching the Truth. While it was perceived to be in "rags" by those who imprisoned him, Bunyan declared that Truth was precious and he would not stop proclaiming it, whether it was politically correct or not. His imprisonment gives evidence that it was not!

Mr. By-ends's response could almost be heard on national television today. He sniffed, "You must not impose . . . Leave me to my liberty." That is the roar in our culture today. Turning our backs on God's protective truth does indeed leave us to our liberty, but it can also lead us to our own destruction!

Oftentimes, those who decide to take seriously the admonition to "stand up, stand up for Jesus, ye soldiers of the Cross"[13] will be leveled with harsh

"You must not impose . . . Leave me to my liberty." That is the roar in our culture today. criticism for not "buying" into political correctness, particularly on the subject of homosexuality. Pejoratives like "knee-jerk, reactionary homophobe" are not all that uncommon (I've heard that a time or two!). But maligning those who will not bend their knee to politically correct ideas is nothing new.

Christian and Hopeful suffered the "slings and arrows" of outrageous criticism for publically aligning themselves with biblical Truth. They were called "overly righteous" and "rigid." They were accused of "condemning all but themselves." Mr. By-ends delivered a stingy indictment when he roared that the two travelers wanted to "hazard all for God." But the red-coated, portly "man of the times" stated that he, instead, would do everything within his power to secure his "life and estate." He says, "I am for religion insofar as the times and my safety will bear it."[14] Sounds like something right out of the twenty-first century! May that *never* be our response! So how should the Church respond to the merchants who are selling twisted ideas in Vanity Fair?

BEING A WINSOME TRAVELER

With prophetic clarity, John Bunyan wrote about the universality of the believer's experience—from the moment we throw off our "backpack" of sin until the day we cross over into the Celestial City. The journey of the travelers, written in the late 1600s, amazingly replicates what is happening in our world today in the twenty-first century. Political correctness was rampant in Bunyan's day as it is in ours. Perversion of the Truth was manifest in Bedford, England, just as it is in America today. While the problem is similar, the solution remains timeless.

As we work our way through Vanity Fair, there are some ways to travel that set us apart from the world. Remember how Christian and Faithful were so easily recognized by the crowd at that noisy fair? They stood out—they were different! Being *in* but not *of* the world should, by design, cause us to be different. That distinction can be manifest in a very clear manner just by the way we talk.

Paul urges us, when engaging the culture, to be *gracious* in the manner in which we communicate: "Let your conversation be always full of grace, seasoned with salt, so that you may know how to answer everyone" (Colossians 4:6 NIV).

It is crucial that we never forget that people who subscribe to beliefs or advance opposing views to what the Bible defines as Truth are *not* our enemies. They may have been caught in the Great Fowler's net, but that does not make them the enemy. I often receive emails from listeners who write with great passion about those who advance sinful worldviews. Their desire to uphold truth in a decaying culture is admirable and right. But often the way they share their perspective would leave the person on the other side of the issue little more than an ink spot on the sidewalk!

We must never forget that our goal, while in the marketplace, is not to make others converts of our opinions but to make Christ known to all.

D. L. Moody would frequently remind believers that they need to be "winsome." Win someone to you, he would say, so we can, in turn, win them to Christ Jesus. We must never forget that our goal, while in the marketplace, is not to make others converts of our opinions but to make Christ known to all. How we deliver His message to the lost is crucial. Minds don't change until hearts change—and the only real and permanent Heart Changer is the Lord. We need to honor Him with both our words and our deeds, even as the merchants shout and taunt. Christian never "returned" fire to his accuser. He addressed Mr. By-ends as "Sir" even though he completely disagreed with him.

There is a second principle that, likewise, cannot be forgotten. God's message must never be watered down to make it more palatable for the Mr. By-ends of the world. Paul cautions us when he says, "My message and my

It is heartbreaking to hear some in the Church today make the declaration that, somewhere along the way, God has changed His mind on the definition of sin.

preaching were not with wise and persuasive words, but with a demonstration of the Spirit's power, so that *your faith might not rest on human wisdom,* but on God's power" (1 Corinthians 2:4–5 NIV, emphasis added).

It is heartbreaking to hear some in the Church today make the declaration that, somewhere along the way, God has changed His mind on the definition of sin. There is a pernicious temptation to "water down" God's Truth because it might just be a bit more "compassionate" or "less judgmental." The Word of God tells us with powerful authority that the captive of sin is set free by Truth. To dilute and distort for political correctness's sake is to keep the captive bound in the chains of sin, and nothing could be more *uncompassionate.*

The difficult challenge we read in Ephesians 4:15 is to speak "the truth *in* love." This is not a multiple-choice test of either Truth *or* love—it is *both* in equal measure. Will it be easy? Absolutely not! That same passage tells us that when we practice this delicate balance of Truth and love, "we will in all things grow up into him who is the Head" (Ephesians 4:15 NIV). In other words, this is a maturing process. Speaking the Truth in love is the very essence of being Christlike. How can we be otherwise?

The problem is that we can sometimes be so hard with the Truth that the "merchants" fail to see the love of Christ in us or in the message we deliver, which makes us anything but winsome. But equally problematic is the challenge not to be so "evan-*jello*-co" that we fail to articulate the Truth of the Word. Silver slippers are always more appealing than rags. But we are not called to define the Truth. Rather, our humbling responsibility is to live out His Truth in our own lives and speak it whenever the Lord opens the door of opportunity.

The Church needs to fling open its doors to anyone who struggles with the area of homosexuality and who wishes to confess his or her sinful behavior, finding forgiveness and healing from God. That is far different from affirming homosexuality or even condoning it, or worse, twisting Scripture to find some tortured justification for sin. It has been said that churches are hospitals for sin-sick souls. We can't allow only the healthy in!

Mr. By-ends will continue to accuse "loving truth-tellers" of being "overly righteous" and "rigid," but that must not deter us on our journey. Marriage is a magnificent picture of God's love for us and of the sacrifice made by His Son. It foreshadows the promise that someday the Bridegroom Himself will return to take us, the Church, His bride, home to be with Him for all eternity! No wonder the Father of All Lies seeks to destroy marriage in this country. The ultimate God-hater hates what Christ has done for us, and marriage is the constant reminder of that unconditional love handed down from the Cross.

The topic of homosexuality can easily make Pilgrims want to pull their collars up around their necks and hope that no one recognizes them in Vanity Fair. The temptation to "duck and cover" is not new. Who likes controversy, and who wants to be rejected? Yet, political correctness is anathema to "speaking the truth in love." May our prayer be the words of Paul, written to the Church at Ephesus. It would have been so easy for this learned man to step back and tone down. That approach could have averted many a beating or imprisonment. But Paul had an encounter with the living God that would forever make him unashamed. The temptation to be PC was there, but being an ambassador for Christ was far more important! May that be both our passion and purpose as well!

> *Pray also for me, that whenever I speak, words may*
> *be given me so that I will fearlessly make known the mystery*
> *of the gospel, for which I am an ambassador in chains.*
> *Pray that I may declare it fearlessly, as I should.*
> Ephesians 6:19–20 NIV

SECTION 4
Faith in Action

How dismal it is to see present day Americans
yearning for the very orthodoxy that their
country was founded to escape.

Christopher Hitchens[1]

Let each citizen remember at the moment
he is offering his vote that he is not making
a present or a compliment to please an
individual—or at least that he ought not so to
do; but that he is executing one of the most
solemn trusts in human society for which
he is accountable to God and his country.

Samuel Adams[2]

I urge, then, first of all, that requests, prayers,
intercession and thanksgiving be made for
all people—for kings and all those in
authority, that we may live peaceful and
quiet lives in all godliness and holiness.

1 Timothy 2:1–2 NIV

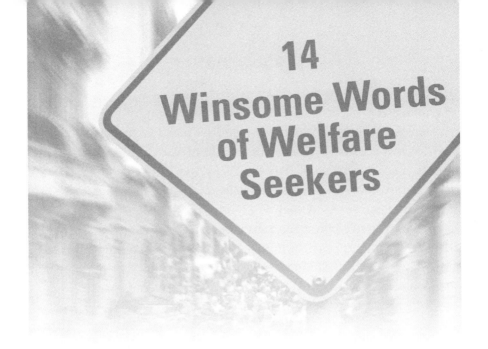

14
Winsome Words of Welfare Seekers

Jeremiah, that weeping prophet, was given a heavy task by God. He was instructed to warn the Israelites that they must not turn back to the wicked ways of their fathers and grandfathers. God's chosen people were strictly forbidden to mix idol worship into the worship of the God of Abraham, Isaac, and Jacob. They were warned that if they disobeyed, disaster would come their way—and it did.

The people of God were led away into captivity in a faraway land. They would be there a long, *long* time. Yet our heavenly Father never turns His back on us, even when we have turned our backs on Him. He used Jeremiah to send a letter of both instruction and comfort.

We have seen how the Israelites were instructed to build homes and plant gardens—to put down roots. They were also told to marry and have children, with instructions that their children were also to marry and continue to multiply in numbers. But the next instruction seems almost counterintuitive, like so much of the letter to the exiles. God directs the people to "seek the welfare of the city where I have sent you into exile, and pray to the Lord on its behalf, for in its welfare you will find your welfare" (Jeremiah 29:7 ESV).

Isn't it interesting how God continues to surprise us (and grow us) by making us think and behave in ways that are radically different from the world around us? The people of God are being instructed actually to pray for those who have taken them into captivity. They are to *intentionally* seek the peace of Babylon. Why? Because the captives' well-being is inexorably tied to the well-being of the captors. That is a radical way of thinking, yet God knew it would protect His people!

But wait, aren't Christians to be completely separate *from* the world? Doesn't "seeking the welfare of the city" create the potential for us to be tainted by the world? Shouldn't we just gather in our "holy huddles" and stay completely away from anything and everyone "out there"?

BIBLICAL ACTIVISM

Fast-forward to the New Testament to find a very interesting man who is the cousin of our Savior. He, like Christian and Faithful, stood out in a crowd. His diet was strange (is there much protein in bugs?), and his clothes would have been featured in the TV show *What Not to Wear*. But John the Baptist was a man completely obedient to God—obedient to the point where it cost him his life.

John was also a political activist. Now before you shout out a roaring rejection of that statement, give me a chance to explain. If we describe political action as any communication or pressure of persuasions brought to bear on those in civil authority in hopes of influencing their values and decisions, then "political" is exactly what this desert prophet was.

Scripture describes three distinct governmental groups that John addressed. First (and wouldn't we all love to talk to this group!), he addressed the tax collectors. Rome was continually levying taxes on its people. There were land taxes and taxes on goods, including slaves. There were import and export taxes at tollbooths and bridges. There was a poll tax on every male over the age of fourteen and on every female over the age of twelve. And collecting taxes was a profitable business.

Tax collectors were the modern-day equivalent of independent contractors. Though they paid Rome the taxes that were demanded, they also regularly overtaxed the people and pocketed the difference. It was a very lucrative way to make a living, but tax collectors were never going to win any popularity awards.

So what did this desert prophet do when he encountered the tax collectors? It is interesting to note that *they* came to John the Baptist. Even tax collectors wanted to be baptized. They met John at the Jordan River and engaged him by asking, "Teacher, what shall we do?" (What a fascinating way to start a conversation!) This was John's golden opportunity to tell them to get out of the dirty *business* of doing *business* with the Roman government. But he did not. Instead, he imparted the ethical rules that were applicable to their political office and in keeping with the kingdom principles he had been sent to preach. John instructed them, "Collect no more than what you have been ordered to" (Luke 3:13 NASB). He was saying, in essence, "If you are in a position of governmental authority, then be honest." His message was clear, concise, honest, and direct. And John knew that if the tax collectors heeded his words, it would benefit everyone. That is seeking the welfare of the city!

But John also encountered a second group—this time it wasn't tax collectors, but soldiers. (Yes, Roman soldiers wanted to be baptized as well.) They too asked the question: "And what about us—what shall we do?" History records that Roman soldiers were often brutal to the civilian population and would many times use their position of power to extort money. Once again, John's directive was clear: "Do not take money from anyone by force, or accuse anyone falsely, and be content with your wages" (Luke 3:14 NASB).

John was instructing those in authority that when you live by kingdom principles, you don't use the power of your position to manipulate others or to frustrate the machinery of justice. And you never use your authority to extort money or favors from those who are subject to you.

The third category of cultural involvement for John the Baptist was the most daunting. Imagine confronting the Jewish head of state, *Herod* himself! Herod's job description was to rule ancient Israel as an arm of the Roman occupation.

The Herod family was definitely not the Waltons! Herod Antipas

(4 BC–AD 39) was the tetrarch who ruled over Galilee during the time of John the Baptist and Jesus of Nazareth. Father Herod Antipas taught his sons to be ruthless. He created in them an insatiable appetite for power. Antipas had learned this lesson at the feet of his father, Herod the Great. He had heard the stories of how his daddy had mercilessly butchered the babies of Bethlehem to destroy any possible threat against his own power and authority.

Those who supported the dynasty of this despicable family were referred to as "Herodians." Nowhere in Scripture do we find any reference to anything good said about either Herod or his followers. Herod Antipas, at the urging of his wife, ordered the execution of John the Baptist. His loyalists also conspired with the Pharisees to destroy Jesus. With the exception of Joseph of Arimathea, Nicodemus, and those unnamed Pharisees who warned Jesus of Herod's plot to kill him (Luke 13:31), there is not one single positive word spoken about Herod or any of his political cronies.

Jesus Himself refers to Herod as "that fox" (Luke 13:32) because of his political craftiness and his deceit. Like any godless politician, Herod's main goal in life was to preserve his power base. How interesting to note that when the Herodians partnered with the Pharisees to entrap Jesus into a damaging position, they used as the primary debating point the issue of taxes (Mark 12:13–15). Taxes were crucial for the continued power of the Roman state and for Herod, the provincial puppet. As we so often see in Washington today, Herod was able to set aside past conflicts with Pontius Pilate, the Roman governor in Judea, when it was necessary for some sort of political gain. The trial of Jesus was a perfect example of their unholy alliance.

Yet this locust-eating prophet, wearing an outfit of animal skins, was fearless in confronting the immorality and corruption of Herod's court. He first denounced Herod's incestuous marriage to Herodias, who was the wife of Philip, his brother (Matthew 14:3–4). That union was clearly condemned in Leviticus 18:16.

But John doesn't stop there. There is the strong sense that the Baptist was also condemning the general corruption that Herod had brought to his office. He was "reproved" by John, not only for his sexual immorality but "because of all the wicked things which Herod had done" (Luke 3:19 NASB). Herod's immorality was a big part of the reason why the nation was not bearing the fruit of righteousness. As a result, judgment was impending. Again with the clarity that comes from being obedient, John delivered a stinging indictment on Herod and on those who aligned themselves with him: "Indeed the axe is already laid at the root of the trees; so every tree that does not bear good fruit is cut down and thrown into the fire" (Luke 3:9 NASB). First-century Israel was that tree, and God was about to cut it down—root, trunk, and branches!

John the Baptist may have been that voice crying in the wilderness, but he was a voice that was heard. His prophetic announcements stressed the imperative of moral absolutes necessary for true kingdom living. John spoke not only to the "common man" but also to those who held positions of authority—from the lowest civil servant to the very head of state. John was seeking the welfare of the city, and no one ever said it would be easy. His proclamations eventually cost him his life.

PAULINE PERSUASION

Aren't you glad that God included the life of Paul in His Word? While Paul was only human, this man's life has been used to teach untold millions how to grow up in Christ. This learned protégé of the rabbi Gamaliel set an example by pressing on, even in the midst of trials and troubles. Paul was never ashamed of the Gospel of Jesus Christ. Beatings, imprisonments, public scorning, and multiple shipwrecks never deterred the apostle's love for the Lord. He had "learned to be content" (Philippians 4:11 NASB); he reminded us that we can "do all things through Christ" because of His strength (Philippians 4:13 NKJV). He brilliantly seized any and every opportunity to proclaim the Truth of God, whether his audience was the Jews or the Greeks. Paul didn't walk—he *waltzed* through the marketplace of ideas.

But he was also Paul, the political activist. In Acts 16:16–40, we read of the account of Paul's illegal arrest. Paul was not only a Jew, he was also a citizen of Rome. Being brilliantly discerning, Paul used his imprisonment as a chance to practice Truth. He had dared to disrupt the corrupt system of the spiritual counterfeits in Philippi. A fortune-teller had been trailing the apostle along his journeys. This clever scam artist used some opportunistic cunning to try to siphon off gullible potential clients who would come to hear Paul. Sadly, we still see charlatans today who try the same thing. I have done many radio broadcasts designed to help listeners learn what the Bible has to say about psychics and astrologers. Incredibly, there are those listeners who defend their use of horoscopes and see no problem with being a Christian and having one's palm read. But there *is* a problem—and Paul knew it. In fact, Scripture says that Paul got "annoyed" with this medium who was able to make contact with demons. With the voice of true authority, Paul commanded "in the name of Jesus Christ" that the demon come out of her. The Bible says, "And it came out that very hour" (Acts 16:18 ESV). Now, *that* is authority.

Paul's action had an immediate economic impact. The local entrepreneurs (Acts 16:19) were livid about their "bottom line" being threatened. Their response was to conspire against Paul and to have him arrested. While their charges were flimsy, they offer the first clue for Paul's defense. "These men are Jews, and they are disturbing our city. They advocate customs that are not lawful for us as *Romans* to accept or practice" (Acts 16:20–21 ESV, emphasis added). The crowd joined in and started to beat Paul and his traveling companion, Silas. Eventually the pair was thrown in jail and their feet put in stocks.

I don't know about you, but I am not sure my first response, while sitting in a filthy jail cell, would have been to have a "praise and worship service"—but that is exactly what Paul and Silas did! They captured the attention of their jailers, who were listening. Paul used his imprisonment to spread the Good News of Jesus Christ (Acts 16:25–32). Classic evangelism in a prison in Philippi! God rocked the earth, and the doors of the jail cell were flung open. The custom of the day was that a jailer was responsible for the security of the prisoner. If a prisoner escaped, the jailer would pay with his life. The door was unlocked as a result of the earthquake, and the jailer assumed that Paul and Silas would try to escape. But they didn't! As they witnessed the jailer grabbing for his sword to take his own life, they shouted for him to stop and not harm himself. This bold act of love caused the man, trembling with fear, to ask, "What must I do to be saved?" The answer given to the jailer is the answer given to us all: "Believe in the Lord Jesus, and you will be saved" (Acts 16:31 ESV). The jailer was baptized (an immediate, public proclamation of his inward transformation), and then he bathed the wounds of his prisoners and fed them both at his own home (Acts 16:33–34). The jailer's entire household believed as well and rejoiced over their newfound faith (Acts 16:34). End of the story? Not at all!

When the word came down from the magistrates that Paul and Silas should be set free, Paul and Silas did not go quietly. The apostle forced the jailers to bring the magistrates down to the jail so they would be exposed to the truth of his unjust imprisonment (Acts 16:37–40). The great and broad Truth of the Gospel was vindicated and demonstrated in the particulars of Paul's protest over the injustice of his illegal jailing.

Paul stood firm for truth: whether it was the broad and universal Truth of salvation through Jesus Christ, or whether it was the particularized truth behind official corruption and mistreatment at the hands of Roman officials. Paul sought the welfare of the city from a prison cell, and lives were eternally changed.

When I tell any truth, it is not for the sake of convincing those who do not know it, but for the sake of defending those that do.
William Blake[3]

If you tell a lie big enough and keep repeating it, people will eventually come to believe it. The lie can be maintained only for such time as the State can shield the people from the political, economic and/or military consequences of the lie. It thus becomes vitally important for the State to use all of its powers to repress dissent, for the truth is the mortal enemy of the lie, and thus by extension, the truth is the greatest enemy of the State.

Joseph Goebbels[1]

As nightfall does not come at once, neither does oppression. In both instances, there is a twilight when everything remains seemingly unchanged. And it is in such twilight that we all must be most aware of change in the air however slight lest we become unwitting victims of the darkness.

William O. Douglas, U.S. Supreme Court Justice[2]

O Lord, who shall sojourn in your tent?
Who shall dwell on your holy hill?
He who walks blamelessly and does
what is right and speaks truth in his heart.

David, Psalm 15:1–2 ESV

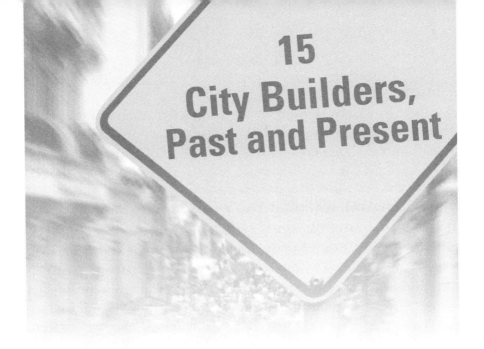

15
City Builders, Past and Present

The word *welfare* has an intriguing meaning. It comes from the Old English phrase *wel faran*, meaning the condition of "being or doing well." What the dictionary doesn't explain is how difficult seeking the "wel faran" of the city can be. Yet, in his letter of instruction to the exiles, that is exactly what the prophet Jeremiah says to the captive: "Seek the welfare of the city."

If we were to be honest with one another, we would have to say that it is so much easier *not* to become involved with the culture of society around us. After all, who wants to get into the muck and mire of a sensate, fallen culture? Isn't it more appealing to stay within the parameters of "the church" with like-minded and like-hearted people where we think we won't hit the trip wire of controversy—where we won't have to stand up and proclaim Truth? Can't one justify not seeking the welfare of the city by simply declaring that "welfare seeking" is not one's area of giftedness? It's a nice try but, as we often say in my beloved commonwealth of Virginia, "That dog don't hunt!" And here's why.

Nowhere in Jeremiah's letter to the exiles does he offer some sort of caveat about *who* is to seek the welfare of the city. It is a general directive to the Israelite captives, and therefore broadly applied to them all. An even stronger argument for cultural engagement is seen in the lives of those who love God and have sought to bring peace and Truth through prayer and action to the world around them. Their stories are recorded, for all time's sake, in Scripture and in the pages of history—and there are many.

A WOMAN WARRIOR AND A FIERCE HOMEMAKER

The hellish concept of blending pagan worship with the worship of Jehovah was a constant threat to the people of God in the Old Testament. As His children began to absorb idolatry and the occult into their culture, they began to realize that, along with this form of syncretism and compromise, they were also becoming oppressed by the Canaanites. Faced with the bitter result of their spiritual betrayal, they "cried out to the Lord" (Judges 3:9 ESV). God heard their prayers and established a series of "judges" who were empowered and directed by the Spirit of the Lord. Their job assignment, commissioned by God, was to provide not only military but also moral deliverance to the people through practical leadership. One of those judges was a woman named Deborah.

The Word of God introduces her as a woman who used to sit under a palm tree on the hills overlooking ancient Ephraim. People would climb the slopes for her judgments. It is under that tree that Deborah was given the message that Barak, one of Israel's military leaders, was to engage the occupying Canaanite army at Mount Tabor. There is something very comforting about going into battle with the assurance that your side will have victory—and that was exactly the case with Deborah (Judges 4:7). But General Barak was a very poor leader, reluctant to follow God's direction as delivered through Deborah. He finally agreed to go to Mount Tabor *only* after Deborah agreed personally to escort Barak and his troops into battle. Now that must have been a sight—10,000 warriors and one woman!

God kept His promise, as He always does, and He routed the Canaanite troops in the wake of Barak's attack and sent their general, Sisera, running for his life. The Bible says that Sisera was to be delivered into the "hand of a woman." Who says God can't use a woman for His good and perfect will? Deborah, as a leader of her people and a welfare seeker for her nation, helped fulfill the work left undone by the death of Joshua.

But the story doesn't end there, as another woman steps out onto the pages of history. Sisera was madly trying to escape the army of Israel, for Barak had been delivered the victory he was promised and "not a man was left" (Judges 4:16 ESV). Sisera felt the troops pressing down on him as he made his way into one of the Israelite tribes that had previously maintained peaceful relations with the Canaanites. He wrongly deduced that he could find sanctuary there. In the midst of that group of people, there sat yet *another* woman. This ancient housewife, a woman named Jael, innocently tended her tent in the midst of military cataclysm. The unsuspecting Sisera was about to encounter one of the great patriots of Israel.

In an absolutely brilliant move of counterintelligence, Jael managed to coax the exhausted Sisera into her home. She offered him a drink of milk and covered his weary body with a rug. He soon nodded off—and Jael moved quickly and softly. She took the implements of her household—a hammer and a tent peg—and with one swift blow drove the stake right into the the side of Sisera's head—a single blow to the temple of Israel's enemy. This little housewife hit him with such force that the peg went through his head and "down into the ground" (Judges 4:21 ESV). This gives new meaning to the phrase, "He never knew what hit him!"

By the time General Barak arrived, there was nothing left to do but celebrate the victory that God had delivered. This military encounter was a turning point in defeating the king of the Canaanites. We read in Judges 5:31 that as a result of the battle, "the land was undisturbed for forty years" (NASB).

Let me offer a special encouragement to women here. Gentlemen, most of you don't struggle in this area, like many women often do. God *still* uses women who work from home, just as He uses women who work outside the home. The story of Deborah and Jael gives clear evidence to that fact. Deborah was the warrior prophetess and Jael the homemaker, but God used them both for His plan and His purpose. Don't let Jael's domestic situation fool you into thinking that she wasn't sharp and discerning as well as obedient. With the common implements of faithfulness in her home, she drove a stake through evil without crossing her front steps. She sought the "welfare of the city" without even leaving home. Hear the words that will forever enshrine her actions: "Most blessed of women is Jael, the wife of Heber the Kenite, most blessed is she of women *in the tent*" (Judges 5:24, emphasis added)

What a wonderful encouragement for women to know that through godly influence on our children and in our households, *and* with the courage to oppose all things opposed to the Lord, we can seek the welfare of the city and be "most blessed . . . of women *in the tent*."

Likewise, Deborah, serving God outside of her tent between Ramah and Bethel, was brave and bold, but most importantly she was obedient. God used her to stir a frightened military man to action. She did great works in God's power and declared the praises of our great and awesome Lord—and in so doing, she sought the welfare of the city!

A QUEEN WHO KNEW HER PLACE IN HISTORY

The Persian Empire exercised the power of occupation over the Jews, with minimal hostilities. Xerxes I, the son of King Darius I, ruled in a world of palace intrigue, where being close to the king could be either a curse or a source of miraculous blessing.

Xerxes had a queen named Vashti who was a stunning beauty. Her name means *best*, which may give us a clue as to where she stood in the harem of wives. One day, after a drinking binge that lasted for seven days, the king decided to show off his beauty queen. He ordered Vashti to make a court appearance, dressed to the nines—crown, jewelry, makeup, *everything*. She refused, and as we read in the book of Esther, Vashti was quickly shown the door. She lost her crown and was banished from the kingdom (Esther 1:19). Being banished turned out to be a better fate for Vashti as Xerxes did not exercise his authority to have her put to death.

But what Xerxes did do, in a burst of chauvinistic bravado, was issue a rather stunning and completely unenforceable decree that must have thrilled henpecked husbands in the kingdom! He pronounced that every man in the land should henceforth be lord and master over his wife (Esther 1:21–22). But in the middle of this robust executive order, Xerxes began to regret banishing his beautiful "best" wife. His counselors, wanting to appease the king, suggested a kind of royal beauty contest among the most beautiful virgins in the land.

In the capital city of Susa lived a man by the name of Mordecai, a Jew and a gatekeeper of the palace. He lived with his young cousin, Esther, whom he had adopted and raised as a daughter. Her description is found in Esther 2:7, where we read that she was "beautiful of form and face" (NASB). Esther was gathered up, along with all the other beautiful virgins of the kingdom, and put into a yearlong spa program in preparation for her presentation to the king.

This breathtaking woman of God stepped onto the stage of history to seek the welfare of the city in a most profound way.

In time, Esther was presented to King Xerxes, and she won him not only with her beauty but also with her kind and gracious spirit. She was crowned queen and took the place (in both the palace and the king's heart) of Queen Vashti. There are no accidents in God's economy. This breathtaking woman of God stepped onto the stage of history to seek the welfare of the city in a most profound way.

Enter an evil man named Haman who could correctly be described as a power-hungry, bureaucratic anti-Semite. He loved to have people bow down before him, but not every knee would bow. Mordecai refused, and an enraged Haman began to plot against God's chosen people. He plotted to annihilate not only the gatekeeper and his family but also the entire Jewish population in the kingdom (stories like this remind us that there really is nothing new under the sun).

Haman began his pernicious campaign by complaining that a "certain people" in the land had "laws (that) are different" and who "do not observe the king's laws" (Esther 3:8 NASB). His crafty argument won the king's approval, and the wheels were put in motion to destroy the Jews. Haman was even given the king's royal signet ring not only to authenticate the death warrant but also to draft and seal his own decree, without Xerxes even seeing it! Copies of the extermination order were sent throughout the land, including a specific date for execution and seizure of all Jewish assets (this does sound so chillingly similar to the demonic actions of Adolf Hitler, doesn't it?).

But God will never allow for the complete extermination of His people. No matter how often Satan tries to eradicate the Jewish people (the people *God* used to bring us His salvation), He will always provide. Five hundred years later, another zealous anti-Semite would be taking the same kind of decree in hand to Damascus. Saul of Tarsus held the authority to arrest, and execute if necessary, any Christians he found in that city. These Christians were mostly converted Jews. In the case of Saul, God intervened in a blinding manner. This man, whose name would soon be changed to Paul, encountered God's own Son on the road to the city, and his heart was changed forever.

However, Haman's heart was a different story. His cold hatred of the Jews had so hardened his heart that God chose to intervene in a different way—this time through a woman.

Mordecai heard of Haman's murderous plan through palace gossip and sought out Esther, urging her to plead with the king to reverse the villainous order. Understandably, Esther was initially reluctant to listen to Mordecai's proposal. Queens entered into the presence of the king *when* the king called. For nearly a month, Esther had not heard from the king. The laws of the land forbade *anyone* from entering into the throne room without a royal invitation. The penalty for disobedience was death. Esther knew that if she followed Mordecai's plan, the possibility of her execution was very real. Seeking the welfare of the city is not necessarily an easy task.

Esther's heart began to change as Mordecai wisely and gently counseled his relative about her crucial place in history and in God's plan. It was no accident that Esther had been chosen by Xerxes in the first place, nor was it an accident that Vashti had been removed. Young, beautiful Esther suddenly found herself in the position of having to approach the most powerful man in the world at that time in order to plead for her people. Mordecai summed up both the situation and the challenge in the most perfect way: "For if you remain silent at this time, relief and deliverance will arise for the Jews from another place and you and your father's house will perish. And who knows whether you have not attained royalty for such a time as this?" (Esther 4:14 NASB). "Esther," he was saying, "one way or another God will rescue His people." Then Mordecai posits the possibility that Esther's head wore a crown because her heart served a greater King.

Esther was convinced. But as she moved to seek the city's welfare, she first asked every Jew in the city to fast before the Lord, as her fellow Jews had a role to play in this as well. The city's welfare was their welfare too. Their prayers and fasting were crucial to what she was about to do. Esther determined to risk everything in order to save her people: "I will go in to the king, which is not according to the law; and if I perish, I perish" (Esther 4:16 NASB). She counted the cost, requested a prayer covering, and obeyed.

Esther did not perish and will forever be remembered for her act of courage. The gallows built for Mordecai's execution took on a different purpose. Xerxes ordered Haman to be hung instead of Mordecai, once the vicious plot was revealed to the king. But he went even further by granting Mordecai an elevated status in the kingdom as well as issuing another official proclamation. This time the executive order granted all the Jews in the kingdom full power of assembly and of self-defense if anyone ever again tried to threaten their existence.

Gracious and fair Esther went from being a young Jewish girl to being the much-favored queen of the land because she had submitted to the Lord's plan for her life. Through her obedience to God, she gained access to the corridors of political power and saved her people from annihilation. Now, *that* is seeking the welfare of the city!

WELFARE SEEKERS WHO CHANGED THE WORLD

History is filled with stories of Christians who have sought the welfare of the city, and in so doing, helped change the world. Consider just a few examples.

William Wilberforce inherited great wealth as a young man and landed in the lap of nobility in England. While traveling through France and Italy with his old schoolmaster, Wilberforce was challenged to read more about what Christ had done for all humankind on the Cross. When he and his teacher returned to England, Wilberforce read the Greek New Testament, and, through the power of the Holy Spirit, the Word of God was secured deep in his heart. Christ had changed his heart, now how would He change Wilberforce's life?

William struggled with whether or not he should stay in politics, having been elected to Parliament at the age of twenty-one. Now a follower of Christ, he thought politics too worldly. It was through his friendship with John Newton, author of one of the most loved hymns of the family of God, "Amazing Grace," that William found his answer. "The Lord has raised you up to the good of his church and for the *good of the nation*," counseled Newton. Newton was encouraging Wilberforce to seek the welfare of the city, and it wasn't going to be easy.

Wilberforce stayed in politics and decided to champion one of the most bitter and contentious issues of his day: the issue of slavery. Like knots in a gold chain, slavery tied itself around almost every economic and financial matter of the day. Members of Parliament were themselves involved in this darkness. Yet Wilberforce knew that God had called him for a purpose, no matter how difficult or daunting the task—and it was *both*!

The first time William introduced a bill in the government to abolish slavery, he spoke for four and a half hours. He was articulate and passionate. History records that it was one of the most moving speeches ever given in Parliament, yet the bill was defeated.

Again Wilberforce introduced a bill, and once again it was defeated. This went on year after year after year. Finally in 1807, twenty years after initially introducing his bill, Parliament passed the bill with an over-whelming majority. Wilberforce received a standing ovation while he sat at his table, face buried in his hands, tears streaming down his face. But the abolition of the slave trade was not the same as the emancipation of the slaves. So Wilberforce pressed on for another twenty years.

This time Wilberforce was not cheered but scorned. Political cartoons made fun of him, his family was threatened, and he was even the victim of an attempted murder. But obedience to God was more important than public acceptance, and he continued his markedly unpopular battle to set the captives free.

Fifty-nine years after William Wilberforce first spoke out against slavery, he would see the fruit of his efforts. He had resigned from Parliament in 1825 and lay on his sick bed in London, not far from the House of Commons. The bill for the emancipation of all the slaves in Great Britain was put to a vote. This time the bill passed. A message was quickly dispatched to Wilberforce who was rapidly ending his pilgrim's progress. On his deathbed, William Wilberforce learned that his lifelong effort had finally come to fruition. Hundreds of thousands of British slaves were now free. William Wilberforce had sought the "welfare of the city," and history was changed forever!

AMERICAN ABOLITIONISTS

America would soon follow what William Wilberforce had started in England. The fuel for the antislavery movement in America came primarily from evangelical Christian fervor.

Three main groups populated the abolitionist position. First, there were the Garrisonians (named after William Lloyd Garrison), radicals and anarchists who held to no particular religious beliefs. The second group was the "political abolitionists," who sought an incremental, political solution out of the slavery controversy. The third group comprised evangelical Christians, and they were the most significant of the three groups. Evangelicals made up more of the leadership of the antislavery movement than any other group.[3]

James McPherson, historian from Princeton University, has noted
the major contributions of the evangelical Church: "The anticlericalism
of Garrisonian abolitionists has obscured the importance of evangelical
Protestantism in the antislavery movement. The revivals of the Second
Great Awakening left in their wake an army of reformers on the march
against sin, especially the sin of slavery."[4]

Seekers of the "welfare of the city" during the abolitionist movement
did not just come from northern states. Whether it was a judge in Georgia warning jurors of the evils of slavery,[5] a pamphlet distributed to the
citizens of North Carolina decrying the selling of fellow human beings,[6]
or a Virginia state representative proclaiming the Golden Rule for all
humankind,[7] Christians lead the way in putting biblical Truth into
action—action that would bring about the end of slavery in America.

AN ARMY OF SALVATION

William Booth was born into a family of means in England in 1829. But
a series of bad business decisions by his father soon left Booth the son
of a poor alcoholic working in a pawnshop. God used that period of his
life to quicken Booth to the needs of the poor and destitute. Booth
became a Christian when he was a teenager and soon discovered he had
the ability to preach, with a passion for evangelism.

One day in 1865, Booth was preaching in London's East End when
some missioners heard him and asked if he would do a series of tent meetings. Booth agreed, the first meeting caused him to realize that he desired,
more than anything else, to serve God by bringing the Gospel to the most
wretched of society, while helping to meet their most basic needs in life.
Booth called the work he was doing "The Christian *Mission.*"

His wife would write that it was common for Booth to arrive home
after a long day of preaching, fatigued and bloodied by stones thrown in
ridicule. Booth would not cave in to discouragement but pressed on for
the "welfare of the city." In 1878, the Christian Mission changed its name
to the Salvation Army, and the work of Booth began to grow explosively.
People were attracted to the idea of being a "soldier" in the army of the

Lord. Those who joined Booth's efforts recognized the battle against darkness and desired to join in the fight. The message of salvation in Jesus Christ coupled with the clear manifestation of Christ's love through humanitarian efforts grew the Salvation Army to the point that, when Booth died in 1912, they were working in fifty-eight countries.[8]

After Booth died, Vachel Lindsay wrote a poem to memorialize the life of the founder of the Salvation Army. The poem was to be sung to the tune of "The Blood of the Lamb." It describes a parade, like those associated with the Salvation Army, but this parade is in heaven, and its celebrants are some of the down-and-out people saved through the ministry of the Salvation Army:

> Every slum had sent its half-a-score
> The round world over. (Booth had groaned for more.)
> Every banner that the wide world flies
> Bloomed with glory and transcendent dyes.
> Big-voiced lassies made their banjoes bang,
> Tranced, fanatical, they shrieked and sang:
> "Are you washed in the Blood of the Lamb?"
> Hallelujah! It was queer to see
> Bull-necked convicts with that land make free.
> Loons with trumpets blowed a blare, blare, blare,
> On, on, upward through the golden air!
> (Are you washed in the Blood of the Lamb?)[9]

Booth viewed the world around him and clearly saw the need for a clear and powerful proclamation of the Gospel. In seeking the welfare of the city, Booth also helped to meet the practical needs of those "bull-necked convicts" who lived in every slum in the world. Booth was obedient to the mandate to engage the world around us for the cause of the Cross, and the world was changed forever. Today the Salvation Army operates in 124 countries, with headquarters in London, England. Lindsay's poem ends by describing Booth's entrance into heaven:

And when Booth halted by the curb of prayer,
He saw his Master through the flag-filled air.
Christ came gently with a robe and crown
For Booth the Soldier, while the throng knelt down.
He saw King Jesus. They were face to face,
And he knelt a-weeping in that holy place.
Are you washed in the Blood of the Lamb?[10]

A MAN OF PRAYER

Before coming to the Lord in the early 1800s, George Ferdinand Müller was known for stealing money, lying, gambling, and drinking. But during his university days, Müller was asked by a friend to attend a Bible study. During one of those studies, Müller saw a man fall to his knees in prayer. That so moved Müller that he too asked Jesus to be his Savior.

Immediately Müller gave up carousing and felt the call to missions and evangelism. He began preaching in local churches, and by his life's end, Müller would have traveled more than 200,000 miles in a world that did not yet know about airplanes.

His biggest passions were Christian education and a love of the Scriptures. He built day schools, Sunday schools, and adult schools, all based on biblical teaching. He founded the Ashley Down Orphanage in Bristol, England, caring for 10,024 orphans during his lifetime.[11] He sought the welfare of the city by caring for children that society had abandoned. He fed not only their empty bellies but their empty hearts at well.

Müller prayed fervently and constantly. His life was filled with stories of God's miraculous answers to prayer. One day the orphanage had no food, but Müller, as was his custom, called all the children to pray and thank God for their food. The children knew there was nothing on the table; Müller knew it as well. But, more importantly, God knew the needs of the children and Müller. After finishing their grace, a baker knocked on the door of the orphanage with more than enough bread to feed all the children. A few minutes later, a milkman delivered buckets and buckets of milk for all of the children. His milk cart had broken down just outside the orphanage, and a prayer was answered. Müller lived a life that exemplified an unwavering belief in a God who provides for all of our needs.

Müller's work in Christian education was built on the Word of God, which he "came to prize . . . alone as [his] standard of judgment." Before going home to glory, Müller had established 117 schools offering Christian education to more than 120,000 children. For George Müller, seeking the welfare of the city started with loving God and His precious Word and manifested itself in serving the least among us by feeding them physically and spiritually. Today, a small museum in Cotham Park, Bristol, England, records the names of all of the children helped as a result of the work of Müller.

A RICH LEGACY OF WELFARE SEEKERS

American history is peppered with examples of people who, in obedience to God, sought "the welfare of the city" and changed forever the direction of our nation. Harvard University, located in Cambridge, Massachusetts, was founded in 1636 and is the nation's oldest institution of higher learning. It was originally established to prepare men for the clergy. Princeton, Brown, Rutgers, and Dartmouth were all started as a direct result of the Great Awakening that spread revival through New England in the eighteenth century.

Christian soup kitchens, Christian hospitals, inner-city missions, homeless shelters, and pregnancy help centers are all a result of believing men and women who have felt that faith in action meant "seeking the welfare of the city" by putting into practice those beliefs that have an immediate and profound effect on the people being served. Showing Christ's love in service to others comes from the wellspring of evangelism. It has never been evangelize *or* engage the culture. It has always been both.

Comforting the hurting, feeding the hungry, clothing the naked, and healing the sick are natural and concrete expressions of the truths replete in Scripture. It is perhaps the very best way to preach the *whole* Truth of the *whole* Gospel to the *whole* world.

America was founded on the idea of separation of powers, limited government, and rights given by God not by a king or elected officials. Our nation was birthed out of the souls of men who sought the welfare of the city using principles derived from the Reformation.

Jeremiah conveyed God's instructions to the Babylonian captives to "seek the welfare of the city." In so doing, the children of God not only helped to protect and prosper themselves, but their captors were beneficiaries as well.

Today, as captives in modern-day Babylon, may we also fervently seek God's face and His leading on how we too may seek the welfare of those around us. May we, like the saints of old, march under the banner of "Engage and Evangelize."

Hear the challenge in these words of William Booth—and join in the march to seek the "city's welfare"!

"Not called!" did you say? "Not heard the call," I think you should say. Put your ear down to the Bible, and hear Him bid you go and pull sinners out of the fire of sin. Put your ear down to the burdened, agonized heart of humanity, and listen to its pitiful wail for help. Go stand by the gates of hell, and hear the damned entreat you to go to their father's house and bid their brothers and sisters and servants and masters not to come there. Then look Christ in the face—whose mercy you have professed to obey—and tell Him whether you will join heart and soul and body and circumstances in the march to publish His mercy to the world.[12]

SECTION 5
Ancient Treachery and Modern Deception

A major function of fundamentalist religion is to bolster deeply insecure and fearful people. This is done by justifying a way of life with all of its defining prejudices. It thereby provides an appropriate and legitimate outlet for one's anger. The authority of an inerrant Bible that can be readily quoted to buttress this point of view becomes an essential ingredient to such a life. When that Bible is challenged, or relativized the resulting anger proves the point categorically.

Bishop John Shelby Spong[1]

Christianity is the greatest intellectual
system the mind of man has ever touched.

Francis Schaeffer[2]

Beware of false prophets, who come to you
in sheep's clothing but inwardly are ravenous wolves.

Jesus, Matthew 7:15 ESV

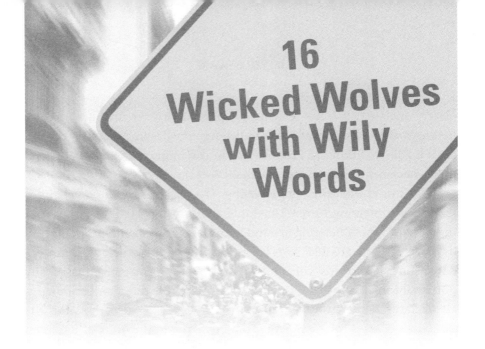

16
Wicked Wolves with Wily Words

Because of their disobedience and idolatry, the children of God found themselves in bondage, living in a strange and faraway land. God, through His prophet, had issued a storm warning, but His people ignored the "weather forecast" and headed into a storm of captivity.

Even when He is disciplining us, God *never* stops loving us. The Bible tells us that He "disciplines the one he loves, and chastises every son whom he receives" (Hebrews 12:6 ESV). In fact, very often the discipline serves as a way to cause us to grow closer to Him, because the disciplining is evidence of God's love for us, His children.

Such was the case with the Babylonian captivity. More than seventy years would pass before the children of God would return home to what today is modern Israel. But while they were living as captives, the Lord provided clear instructions on how to not simply exist but *thrive*. He delivered His message through His prophet Jeremiah.

The letter to the exiles instructed them to build homes, plant gardens, marry, have children, and encourage their children to marry. They were also given directions to seek the welfare of the city for the sake of their captors as well as themselves. But the letter, found in Jeremiah 29 goes on to add one more instruction—one very different from the other directives they had been given. The Lord of hosts, the God of Israel, then clearly declares, "Do not let your prophets and your diviners *who are among you* deceive you, and do not listen to the dreams that they dream, for it is a lie that they are prophesying to you in my name; I did not send them, declares the Lord" (Jeremiah 29:8–9 ESV, emphasis added).

Don't miss what the Lord is saying. The deceivers are *in their midst!* God is not referring to the Babylonians but rather He is talking about the false prophets hanging around with the captives. The prophets and the diviners who are deceivers are living among the exiles, and they are dangerous. Up to this point in the letter, God has not addressed any potential threats the exiles might face. But now He does, and the threat, He declares, comes from *within!*

God does not tolerate lying prophets. Early in the book of Jeremiah (chapter 14) the Lord warns again about those who falsely prophesy in His name. "I did not send them, nor did I command them or speak to them. They are prophesying to you a *lying* vision, *worthless* divination, and the *deceit of their own minds*" (Jeremiah 14:14 ESV, emphasis added). God leaves no question as to where He stands on the issuing of wolves among the sheep.

As we wander through the marketplace of ideas, the "streets" are filled with booths where lying "merchants" are offering worthless goods based on the deceit of their own arrogant and markedly unbiblical thinking. This may be one of the most daunting and troublesome parts of Vanity Fair. Here is where sheep are led astray by attractive and charismatic wolves, but they *are* wolves nonetheless. Here, dear "buyer," is where we must be *very* aware.

So what are the signs of a false prophet? The answer that applied to the Babylonian captives still applies to us today. First, they are not sent *by* God. Second, their message is not *from* God but rather contains a "false vision." Third, they are suffering deceptions of their own minds. This last point is crucial. These wolves may have actually deluded themselves into believing *their* word is the Word of God. But the ultimate test is this: Does their message line up with the Word of God? If it does not, then the message of the prophet is false, not the other way around.

Paul instructs his young student Timothy in this area when he writes that God's Word (the Bible) provides wisdom leading to salvation. It will "make you wise for salvation through faith in Christ Jesus" (2 Timothy 3:15 ESV). He goes on to tell Timothy that not only is all Scripture "God-breathed," but it is profitable for our daily walk. It provides teaching, reproof, correction, and training for righteousness (2 Timothy 3:16).

The Word of God builds us up with the straight stick of Truth and puts us on solid ground, where our hearts will never collapse under the weight of ugly lies and deception.

False teachings can't do that. But the Bible does something else: It builds us up.

When we think of equipment for building we think of hammers, saws, nails, levels—all of the tools someone working in construction might need. Paul teaches us that the Word of God "equips" (builds us) for the work that the Holy Spirit is to do through us. False teachings in our lives are like crooked tape measurers and rusty nails. You might be able to use such tools to create a temporary building of some sort, but the structure will eventually decay and collapse. The Word of God builds us up with the straight stick of Truth and puts us on solid ground, where our hearts will never collapse under the weight of ugly lies and deception.

VOICES OF DECEPTION

The *first* great lie was uttered in the garden of Eden, when the Father of *All* Lies slithered up to Eve. Described as "more crafty" than any other beast, the "serpent" began his first conversation with a human being by asking a question that calls into account the authority and the inerrancy of the Word of God: "Did God *actually* say . . . ?" (Genesis 3:1 ESV, emphasis added). What a way to begin a conversation! The first words this about-to-be disobedient mortal heard was that maybe, *just maybe*, God's Word isn't all it's cracked up to be. The Liar then took the very words of

God, twisted them around, and stood them on their head. "God knows that when you eat of [the fruit of the tree of the knowledge of good and evil] your eyes will be opened, and you will be like God" (Genesis 3:5 ESV). What a wonderful idea, Eve thought. "Maybe God didn't really mean what He said, or maybe I need to find some meaning in His words that have more personal relevance to where I am in life. Maybe His ideas are a bit old-fashioned and not really appropriate for such a modern woman like me. The tree was good for food, it was appealing to the eyes, and it would make one wise. It doesn't get any better than that," she rationalized, and she didn't hesitate. "Pass me the fruit!" The serpent hissed in delight, Eve bit, and sin came into the world. The Great Deceiver had snagged his first victim, but it surely wouldn't be his last. "When he lies, he speaks out of his own character, for he is a liar and the father of lies" (John 8:44 ESV).

Crafty lies are still being sold and, unfortunately, bought in the marketplace. They tend to come in rather sophisticated forms and shapes, replete with praise from powerful secular entities. Take, for example, Bruce Bawer. He is considered a cultural critic, and his essays have appeared in publications like the *New York Times* magazine. But he also wrote a book entitled *Stealing Jesus: How Fundamentalism Betrays Christianity*. In the book, Bawer posits

Call me narrow-minded, but somehow I just can't imagine a metaphor offering fruit to Eve, can you?

that what he calls "legalistic Protestantism" sees "truth" as something established in the Bible and known for sure by true Christians. On the other hand, "nonlegalistic Protestantism" reads the Bible with more critical thinking, intelligence, and an understanding of the historical and cultural context of what the Scriptures say.[3]

For Bawer, believing that God's Word *is* revealed Truth that can be universally understood by those who read it is being narrow-minded. He considers that those who think only God can ever know Truth and we need the Bible and other historical and religious texts to "point the way" are more open-minded. The author further contends that "legalistic Christians" *mistakenly* believe that Jesus' "chief purpose was to carry out the mission of atonement." Open-minded (or perhaps closed-minded, depending on your perspective) Christians believe that Jesus' main goal was to show that God loves all people and that "all humankind is one." Narrow-minded Christians think the devil is real; open-minded Christians think he is a metaphor.[4] Call me narrow-minded, but somehow I just can't imagine a metaphor offering fruit to Eve, can you?

Bawer goes on to make yet another outlandish statement, this time dealing with the mandate for sound doctrine. Using a character out of Frank Peretti's bestselling book *This Present Darkness*, Bawer says that a preacher in the novel uses a passage that is a "favorite" of legalistic Protestants. In 2 Timothy 4:2–4 Paul instructs his student, young Timothy, to preach the Word and to be ready to do so both in and out of season. He instructs, "Reprove, rebuke, and exhort, with complete patience and teaching. For the time is coming when people will not endure sound teaching, but having itching ears they will accumulate for themselves teachers to suit their own passions, and will turn away from listening to the truth and wander off into myths" (ESV). Bawer contends that this message of Paul's is not a part of the "Gospel."[5] This is both convenient and paradoxical.

There are three reasons why this contention is erroneous. First, Paul was personally commissioned by Jesus on the road to Damascus (Acts 9:3–9). The Good News was directly delivered to Paul, and the Gospel was a message forever branded into what Paul preached. Second, Paul's letters are verified as part of Scripture by Peter. In 2 Peter 3, the author wrote about Paul and mentioned "the wisdom given him, as he does in all his letters" (2 Peter 3:15–16 ESV). That wisdom came from the Lord, breathed by the Holy Spirit, and written down by man—every word inspired, every word God-breathed, all part of the Gospel message.

Peter went on to make a statement that would make Bruce Bawer squirm. The big fisherman wrote these words: "There are some things in them [Paul's letters] that are hard to understand, which the ignorant and unstable *twist to their own destruction*, as they do the other Scriptures" (2 Peter 3:16 ESV, emphasis added). Paul's writings are a part of Scripture, a part of God's Word, a part of the Good News for humankind.

Finally, Paul's letters explain the meaning of the Gospel message over and over again. He tells us *why* Christ came, the reason He died, what He did for humankind, and how we are to live like Him. Bawer does not believe that "the Gospel" is found in every part of the New Testament. That narrow thinking falls into the same category of believing that the only part of the New Testament that applies to us are those words some Bible publisher decided to print in red. We either take all of Scripture as Truth from the first word of Genesis to the last sentence of Revelation, or we take none of it. A. W. Tozer summed up this point perfectly when he said, "The Word of God well understood and religiously obeyed is the shortest route to spiritual perfection. And we must not select a few favorite passages to the exclusion of others. Nothing less than a whole Bible can make a whole Christian."[6]

> **We either take all of Scripture as Truth from the first word of Genesis to the last sentence of Revelation, or we take none of it.**

A JESUS SEMINAR WHERE JESUS IS ABSENT

Doctrinal heresy is not a new problem for the Church. How fascinating that as far back as 586 BC, God, through His prophet Jeremiah, was warning His people to be careful of false prophets in their midst. It comes as no surprise that for the past 100 years, liberal theologians and academics have advanced something called "The Quest for the Historical Jesus." In truth, it is not a quest at all, but rather an attempt to mold and shape the Son of God into a more manageable, more mortal character while at the same time explaining away the miraculous. These so-called debunkers claim that the four Gospels of Matthew, Mark, Luke, and John are the writings of men who lived hundreds of years after Jesus and who have embellished the stories of the Messiah. The endgame is to strip away anything supernatural that cannot be explained through the grid of their scientific, anti-supernatural bias. What remains after all of the whittling and sanding is a Jesus of their own creation. Such "de-constructors" join the ranks of men like Voltaire, Thomas Paine, Thomas Jefferson, and Bertrand Russell.

What is different this time, with these modern merchants of shabby goods, is that the appeal of conversion to heresy is being made directly to the churches of America. They call their gatherings the "Jesus Seminars" and hold meetings around the country from California to Washington, DC. The founder of the Jesus Seminars, sponsored by the Westar Institute, was Robert Funk, who died in 2005. He worked diligently to reeducate Christians on the meaning of Christ. One of his books, *The Acts of Jesus*, claimed to be "the search for the authentic deeds of Jesus."[7]

The book uses a unique color-coding system. Like the "red letter" editions of the Bible, *The Acts of Jesus* is a kind of "red letter" book for skeptics. Those parts of the Gospels that are "unequivocally" accurate representations of who Jesus really was are put in *red*. Those parts that *may* be accurate, according to the liberal scholars, are in *pink*. The parts of the Gospels that may have some relevance to the real Jesus, but which these skeptics think were not part of the original information that the disciples had about Jesus are put in *gray*. And, last, those parts considered inaccurate accounts of Christ are left to standard *black* print. Can you guess which color dominates? If you said a mass of black, with very few red or pink passages, you would be correct. According to these false prophets, only 16 percent of the Gospel events are deemed to be accurate and only 18 percent of the Gospel sayings of Jesus can be reliably attributed to Him.

Here's an example. John 3:1–21 is a hugely important passage of Scripture, where we read of the meeting between Jesus and Nicodemus, a Pharisee who had been secretly impressed with Jesus and who had been watching Him from afar. Nicodemus slips into Christ's camp one night to talk with Him. Jesus tells the Pharisee (and all who read that passage) that one can only see the kingdom of God if he is "born again." Nicodemus is bewildered at the response and Jesus goes on to explain, "For God so loved the world, that he gave his only Son, that whoever believes in him should not perish but have eternal life. For God did not send his Son into the world to condemn the world, but in order that the world might be saved through him" (John 3:16–17 ESV).

According to Robert Funk and his associates at the Jesus Seminars, this entire account is neither accurate nor historical. In fact, Nicodemus, they proffer, is a made-up character in a pretend dialogue that never happened. The entire episode was written, they argue, to symbolize some theological truth, not a historical reality.

Think about what Funk and his cohorts are asking us to "buy." These deceivers make the flawed and false assumption that the early believers in Jesus treated theological truth as something different from actual events that happened in history. They ask us to believe that these first-century saints were willing to be tortured, be thrown to the

These men and women of the faith didn't give up their lives just for a good idea!

lions, suffer crucifixion, and die as martyrs for what was, in fact, not true but only appeared to be true in some fuzzy theological sense. These men and women of the faith didn't give up their lives just for a good idea! They lived and died for Truth—transcendent, absolute, and perfect. The Christian martyrs did not die for a leader whose body was still in the tomb—they gave their lives because the tomb was and still remains empty.

KILLING TRADITIONAL FAITH BY CREATING A NEW ONE

Paul made rather a stunning comment to Timothy in his first letter to his young pupil. He wrote, "Now the Spirit expressly says . . ." (1 Timothy 4:1 ESV). Stop for a moment and ponder the seriousness of this pronouncement. Paul wanted Timothy to know that what he was about to say is not up for debate in academic circles on some Ivy League campus somewhere. Rather, the warning he would give is so crucial that it had been given several times before in Scripture. It is the exact same warning given to the elders at Ephesus (Acts 20:29–30). The message: *Be aware of apostasy!* The Holy Spirit is telling us, "Look out! There are wolves out there! Be careful and be watchful!"

I take great comfort in this warning. It reminds me there truly is "nothing new under the sun." The Great Deceiver continues to rattle his tail to this day and steadily asks us, "Has God really said?" He made Eve question God in the garden, and he continues to try to make us question God today. The mere fact that Satan continues to deceive gives further credence to the power and authority of God's Word! The Liar must continue to lie because Truth remains the enduring Truth.

Paul continues, "In later times some will depart from the faith by devoting themselves to deceitful spirits and teachings of demons, through the insincerity of liars whose consciences are seared" (1 Timothy 4:1–2 ESV). My, what a politically incorrect statement! Let Paul's words serve to remind us that boldness is as much a part of the faith as is humility.

Paul's words remind us that these false teachers will always be among us. There will be some who will fall prey to these apostates, and they *will* walk away from the Truth. We are instructed to be careful not to fall into this deception.

John Shelby Spong, the bishop of the Episcopal Diocese of Newark, New Jersey, until his retirement in 2001, has sold millions of his books. His website describes him as a "champion of inclusive faith."[8] His book titles give a strong indication of his worldview regarding the inerrancy of Scripture and the Word of God: *The Sins of Scripture* and *A New Christianity for a New World*. Spong doesn't take a holistic approach to the Bible but rather chooses to reinterpret the Word into a more modern, more *inclusive* kind of theology. He picks and edits what he does and does not believe the Scriptures say rather than identifying all of the Bible as having been "God-breathed" (2 Timothy 3:16 NIV).

In his writings, Spong has correctly listed what have historically been considered the basic fundamentals of Christianity. They are, in the following order:

The inspiration of Scripture as the literal, revealed Word of God

The Virgin Birth

The substitutionary view of the atonement, accomplished by the
     death of Christ

The bodily resurrection of Jesus

The Second Coming of the Lord[9]

But Spong then shows himself to be a wolf in sheep's clothing by making the statement that, for him, these fundamentals are "not just naïve, but eminently rejectable."[10] He also alleged that none of these basics of orthodox Christianity can be supported by modern reputable "Christian" scholars. In a speech delivered in Berkeley, California, at the Graduate Theological Union, Spong said, "Surely the essence of Christianity is not found in any or all of these propositions."[11]

In his attempt to "modernize" Scripture to be more inclusive, Spong argues that attitudes about what is moral and immoral have changed with the times. Hence, homosexuality is not considered a sin when seen in a *modern* context. He also posits that the virgin birth, physical resurrection of Jesus, and the second coming are merely theological symbols. *Merely symbolic?* Tell that to the more than five hundred witnesses who saw Jesus after He had died and then rose again. And after the crucifixion and the bodily resurrection of Jesus, how did the apostles have breakfast on the shore of the Sea of Galilee with a "symbol"? But even more repulsive is Spong's take on the completed work of Calvary. He views the substitutionary work of the Cross as "grotesque."[12] If this core belief is a part of biblical orthodoxy, then, Spong says, it has rendered Christianity hopelessly unbelievable.

Watchman Nee, whose real name was Nee Tao Shu, was a Christian in China who ministered in that country for more than thirty years. More than 2,300 home churches were established because of his efforts for the kingdom. He was arrested for his public profession of faith in 1952 and would eventually lose his life in prison, twenty years later. At the time of his death, a note was found under his pillow in prison that said: "Christ is the Son of God. He died to atone for men's sin, and after three days rose again. This is the most important fact in the universe. I die believing in Christ."[13]

Either Watchman Nee is correct and what Jesus did for us *is* the most important fact in the universe, or John Shelby Spong is correct and what Jesus did for us is "grotesque" and "unbelievable." They both *can't* be right. Welcome to the marketplace of ideas! This is such a profound example of what is being bought and sold in the public square—and the consequences of the "purchase" of these "goods" is stunning. The acceptance of Spong's ideas leads to eternal separation from God but acceptance of what Nee preached results in eternity in His presence.

More recently the battle for biblical truth took a new turn. Rob Bell's book entitled *Love Wins: A Book about Heaven, Hell, and the Fate of Every Person Who Ever Lived*, created a firestorm both inside and outside the church in America.[14] Leaders in the emerging church defended Bell and declared that the idea of hell and eternal separation from God simply couldn't be defended anymore. In other words, we have matured, become more sophisticated, and outgrown an outdated concept. Sounds a bit like Spong, doesn't it?

But there's that issue of the Bible again. If the idea of hell is in transition, if we need to modernize our thinking to be more inclusive, more relevant, and more compassionate, then we are going to have to do away with what Jesus Himself said in Matthew 5:22 ESV ("the hell of fire"), Matthew 5:29 ("whole body thrown into hell"), Matthew 10:28 ESV ("soul and body in hell"), Matthew 25:46 ("eternal punishment"), and Mark 9:45–47 ESV ("be thrown into hell"). And these are just a few examples. Then there are Peter (2 Peter 2:4) and Paul (2 Thessalonians 1:8–9) and more than eighty verses in the New Testament on the topic of hell.

The question of hell calls into account the very nature of salvation—and that too is questioned by Bell. He writes: "Will everyone be saved, or will some perish apart from God forever because of their choices? Those are questions, or more accurately, those are tensions we are free to leave fully intact. We don't need to resolve them or answer them because we can't, and so we simply respect them, creating space for the freedom that love requires."[15] Either Rob Bell is right on the concept of hell or Jesus Christ is right, but they can't *both* be right.

"Buy, buy, *buy!*" shout the merchants in Vanity Fair. But a cautionary note is crucial as we enter the city square, for many of the goods are deadly and are being hawked by false prophets and deceivers among us. The Bible warns us to be cautious, careful, and discerning. We are to know what we believe and why we believe it and then be prepared to enter the marketplace of ideas *ready and able* to give a reason for the "hope that is in [us]" (1 Peter 3:15 ESV). Our basis of understanding and our knowledge of the Truth come from God's Word. We haven't outgrown it like an old pair of shoes. It doesn't need to fit into a more modern context because its Truth transcends the ages. It remains the ultimate definition of *inclusive* as its precepts and principles apply to all people, in all times, and in all places.

As problematic as false prophets were and still are today, there is yet another group of deceivers Jeremiah goes on to discuss in his letter to the Babylonian captives. These he calls the "diviners." This time, the attack comes not from *inside* the Church, through false teachers, but from *outside* the Church. Our journey is going to get even more intriguing so tighten the straps on your sandals, adjust your backpack, and let's continue, fellow Pilgrim.

*If you believe what you like in the Gospel and reject what you
do not like, it is not the Gospel you believe, but yourself.*
Augustine

I stand back detached and I can hear the spirit person
I am channeling, but I can't hear it clearly—and then
suddenly it goes blank, that's really when they are in.

Derek Acorah[1]

If the whole universe has no meaning, we should
never have found out that it has no meaning: just as,
if there were no light in the universe and therefore
no creatures with eyes, we should never know
it was dark. Dark would be without meaning.

C. S. Lewis[2]

There shall not be found among you anyone who burns
his son or his daughter as an offering, anyone who practices
divination or tells fortunes or interprets omens, or a
sorcerer or a charmer or a medium or a necromancer
or one who inquires of the dead, for whoever does
these things is an abomination to the Lord.

Deuteronomy 18:10–12 ESV

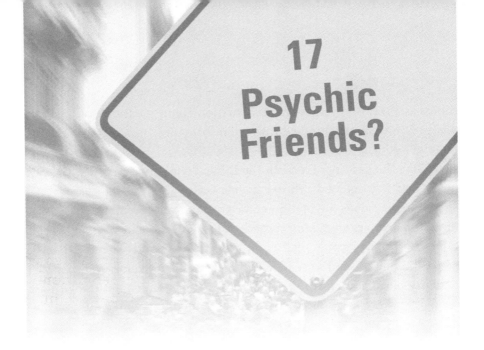

17
Psychic Friends?

For a long, long time, God has been telling His children, whether they were captives in Babylon or captives in a sin-sick fallen world, to stay away from the occult, in all of its various shapes and forms. And yet, not unlike Eve drawn to the tree whose fruit she was forbidden to eat, far too many men and women of God get dangerously close to this prevalent darkness.

In his letter to the exiles, the prophet Jeremiah warned the people that they are to be watchful and to stay away from two types of threats: false prophets and diviners. He told them these wolves are in "their midst." In other words, they don't need to go looking for trouble; trouble will find them. With clarity, Jeremiah said, "Your prophets and your diviners who are *among* you deceive you" (Jeremiah 29:8 ESV, emphasis added). False prophets work their way into the Church while diviners like to surround the Church.

But there is a significant distinction between the false prophets and the diviners. We have already taken a look at the false prophets, so let's discover, here in this bustling marketplace of ideas, who these diviners are and why they are so effective in selling their wares.

Diviners practice the art of divination. Broadly defined, *divination* means the practice of consulting people (living or dead) or consulting things as a way of trying to get information about the future or life after death. The term also implied that the information comes from a being, like the Pythia who delivered the oracle at Delphi or from some occurrence like the casting of lots. In the Bible, divination is associated with magic and was deemed a threat against Israel.

In ancient days, divination came through various methods. Sometimes the diviners would interpret dreams by sleeping in a pagan temple. Other times, they would read a horoscope of the stars, believing that the earth and humankind were in harmony with the universe. Another particularly pernicious form of divination involved consultation with the dead. The message would come through a medium, who would receive it from a "familiar spirit."

Another occult practice was to study the entrails of animals, particularly the livers. The liver was once considered the basis of life and was often used in animal sacrifices. The captives would have heard much about this type of divination as it was widely used by the Babylonians. Hiccups, sneezing, and the movement of animals were also interpreted and used as tools in the work belt of the diviner. But what was not a part of their toolkit was the Word of God. Divination was about pagan practices—pure and simple. And these practitioners are turning quite a profit today.

Jeremiah, speaking the words of God, used the words, "your diviners," meaning that the children of God had brought occult influences into their midst, *by themselves* and of their own volition. Regrettably, some in the Church are doing the very same thing today. Here, ignorance is no excuse.

The Old Testament records multiple occasions when God's people are told to not have anything to do with the occult, no matter how harmless it might appear at first. In Leviticus 19:26, the directive from God to Moses starts with the words, "You shall not." If our mom or dad gave us a directive that started with those words, we would not have a problem understanding exactly what they meant and what we were forbidden to do. With continued clarity, God tells Moses that there is to be *no* fortune-telling or interpretation of omens. In Deuteronomy 18:9–14, God gives Moses a list of abominable practices that the Israelites are prohibited from participating in such as using mediums, necromancers or sorcery.

During the reign of King Saul, the use of occult practices to communicate with the dead was something done not just by the king but by the people as well. They knew that Saul had used a medium from Endor to try to make contact with the prophet Samuel who had died. The people also knew this was strictly forbidden, which is why the prophet Isaiah reminded them, "And when they say to you, 'Inquire of the mediums and the necromancers who chirp and mutter,' should not a people inquire of their God?" (Isaiah 8:19 ESV). You have to love the phrase *chirp and mutter*. Today people actually pay hard-earned money for the chirps and mutterings by calling a 900 number or visiting a website. Can't you hear the merchants shouting, "We sell chirps and mutterings! Buy, buy, *buy!*"

The warnings and the admonitions don't stop with the Old Testament. The New Testament carries this message forward in several places. In Acts 13:6–12, Dr. Luke recorded how the apostle Paul faced down Elymas (his name actually means "magician"), who was practicing divination as well as attempting to turn the Roman governor on the island of Cyprus away from the faith. Paul stared him down through the power of the Holy Spirit, calling Elymas the "son of the devil" and the "enemy of all righteousness" and someone "making crooked the straight paths of the Lord" (ESV). Paul eventually leads the proconsul to faith, in spite of the magician's attempts. Acts 16:16 tells how Paul exorcized a "spirit of divination" from a young girl. We also read about Simon, the sorcerer who caused chaos and confusion in Samaria.

Readers and believers of the Bible are without excuse. We are to have nothing to do with these diviners who are a real and present danger to the Church today, just as they were in the days of Jeremiah. So how do we recognize these modern-day sorcerers? It's not hard. Walk into any general market bookstore and look for the "religion" section. More often than not, you will find more books on the New Age movement, or mysticism or horoscope reading, than you will find Bible commentaries or devotionals. Unfortunately, more and more of the diviners' names are becoming recognizable because of the platforms they are being given through mass media.

MODERN MEDIUMS AND SLIPPERY SOOTHSAYERS

Deepak Chopra is often referred to as a leader in the field of mind-body science. He has his own radio show, writes columns that appear in major newspapers, has written more than sixty-four books, and appears regularly on the Public Broadcasting System. He often weaves words from advanced physics into his explanation of who we are in the universe and the connection between our bodies and spirits and the world around us—words like "event horizon."

Chopra's website states that one of his books, *War of the Worldviews: Science vs. Spirituality*, "successfully elevates the conversation between science and religion in a way that is thoughtful and constructive rather than polarizing and divisive" (another example of our postmodern culture demanding tolerance over Truth).[3] He will frequently use Bible verses as a way to advance some of his ideas, but invariably those passages will be taken out of context and their meanings called into account. For example, using Matthew 7:7 as his frame of reference ("Ask, and it will be given to you; seek, and you will find," ESV), Chopra believes that being "born again" is actually a form of "second attention." This is a kind of mental peripheral vision, where we find God intuitively and inwardly, picking up God's clues as a mind reader might discover someone else's thoughts.[4]

In his book *The Third Jesus*, Chopra takes several New Testament verses and then superimposes them with Eastern mysticism. He challenges the reader to see what Jesus says in the "light of a higher consciousness." He believes that Christianity is laden with impossible expectations, among them the belief that God forgave all sins through Jesus. Rather, he teaches that "forgiveness" is a process, which is more in keeping, he thinks, with spiritual growth.[5] To back up his ideas, he quotes from the Book of Thomas, and therein lies yet another problem.

Sprinkling a little **Scripture here and there, and covering it with a layer of narcissism and mysticism, in the end creates a financially lucrative formula. But it is also eternally lethal.**

The Book of Thomas is not in the New Testament. Rather it is part of the dubious Gnostic Gospels, which are not inspired, were rejected by the early Church, and were probably written one or two hundred years after the life of Christ. The authors are unknown, and the writings are filled with occult philosophy. But, if you want personal revelation according to Chopra, then you must see the Gnostic Gospels in the light of what he often refers to as the "higher consciousness."[6] If someone reaches God-consciousness, then, according to this diviner, you will experience revealed truth. Sprinkling a little Scripture here and there, and covering it with a layer of narcissism and mysticism, in the end creates a financially lucrative formula. But it is also eternally lethal. Can you hear the serpent again, asking if what God has said is true?

Another proponent of this same kind of thinking is Neale Donald Walsch. He is the founder of ReCreation, a spirituality and "personal growth" foundation. Like Chopra, he bathes his theories with biblical-sounding ideas. He too refers to "Christ-consciousness" but his teachings bear no resemblance to the concept of Scripture that teaches us that in Christ, we have a renewed mind because of our personal relationship with Jesus. Rather Walsch talks about a kind of super-consciousness, where our minds and emotions are "fully integrated," and we are "fully creative." Truth, he believes, is *created*, not discovered. He "discovered" (or rather created) truth through channeling, an occult practice. His book *Conversations with God*, volume one, was on the *New York Times* list for ninety-one weeks and was translated into twenty-seven languages. Soothsaying has always been a profitable business.[7]

But perhaps the most successful diviner of all is one of the most powerful, wealthy, and influential women in the world today.

THE DIVINE MISS "O"

From her time as an obscure television reporter in Baltimore, Maryland, to her ascension as a nationally syndicated radio and TV host, Oprah Winfrey's story of success is legend. Having ended her daily television program in 2011, Oprah now runs an entire network called The Oprah Winfrey Network or OWN. Regardless of the size of her platform, her ideas and worldview have remained the same and have a global impact.

Having been turned off at an early age by the concept of God being a "jealous" God (Exodus 20:5) and not really understanding what that means in terms of the Lord loving us so deeply and so unconditionally, Oprah began a journey of spiritual self-construction. Part-New Age, part-pantheistic, part-Christian, Oprah's "religion" is remarkably "me"-centric. Regardless of how it is labeled, what she is selling is dangerous.

One of the ways Oprah "evangelizes" is by getting her message out through various media. She will often conduct "classes" online as a way of introducing leaders in the New Age movement. People like Deepak Chopra, Iyanla Vanzant, and Marianne Williamson have become household names as a result of their association with Oprah.

Take, for example, Oprah's conversations with Eckhart Tolle. Tolle, a self-taught spiritualist, has been identified by the *New York Times* as "the most popular spiritual teacher in the [United States]."[8] Tolle's book *A New Earth: Awakening to Your Life's Purpose* skyrocketed to the top of the bestseller lists almost as a direct result of doing a series of webinar interviews with Oprah. Thirty-five million people are believed to have tuned in while Tolle shared his ideas of the "One Consciousness," and people in record numbers literally *bought* the lie.[9] And it's not surprising considering that the Gospel according to Tolle is all about *you*—"me-ism" at its highest level!

In his book *A New Earth*, he writes that the truth is really inseparable from each one of us. But he goes on to say that *you* are the Truth (and yes, he does capitalize the *t*) He explains:

> The very Being that you are is Truth. Jesus tried to convey that when he said, "I am the way and the truth and the life." These

words uttered by Jesus are one of the most powerful and direct pointer to the Truth, if understood correctly. If misinterpreted, however, they become a great obstacle. Jesus speaks of the innermost I Am, the essence identity of every man and women, every life-form, in fact. He speaks of the life that you are.[10]

Satan trapped Eve and told her that if she would just eat—just taste the fruit of the Tree of the Knowledge of Good and Evil (something God told her expressly not to do)—she would be like God Himself. The "Father of All Lies" needed to lie to deceive her; he focused on the primacy of "self" to woo her to disobedience. Today, that same lie is still being told. "You shall be like God!" Satan is clever and sticks with a plan that works. Making us believe we are the center of the universe—that the world revolves around us—has been a lie effectively used by the Chief Deceiver since we walked out of the garden.

Oprah has successfully advanced the fallacy that we are either god or victim or perhaps both.

Oprah has successfully advanced the fallacy that we are either god or victim or perhaps both. Oprah's "god" message comes in the form of self-help advisors who promote the concept that by "thinking" we "become" whatever it is we want to be. If that were the case, all sick people could "wish" themselves into good health (Paul might have tried that if it worked for his "thorn in the side") and people who are struggling financially could "wish" themselves into wealth. The idea that we are the *makers* of our own destiny, the *captains* of our own ships, and the *creators* of our own future contains one small element of truth while utterly denying the authority, power, and sovereignty of an almighty God.

Oprah's history of broadcasts is filled with stories of people who have been victims of one kind or another. Those kinds of messages come through the television screen loud and clear to a world filled with brokenness and pain. But there is also a problem with that message. Dr. Eva Illouz, a

The idea of **victimhood plays well into the hands of women, in particular, who think that being born female instead of male is a burden that must be carried through life.**

sociologist at Hebrew University has been quoted as saying that Oprah has turned suffering into something to be exalted—and all suffering should be used as a vehicle for improving one's self.[11] Therefore, suffering is a desirable experience.

C. S. Lewis' statement that God whispers to us in our pleasures but shouts to us in our pain[12] serves to remind us that Our Father can and does use adversity to mold and shape us to the image of His Son. But the molding and shaping is done not by us but by the God who loves us and made us. Change happens when we are willing to surrender to His will. Suffering becomes beneficial in the life of the believer when it is seen as a conduit for transformation in our lives—not because of what we do but because of what we can't do. Surrender is victory, and that is the message the world does not understand. The modern-day "diviners" sell the shabby goods of "thinking equals being" and the idea that each of us can self-determine the outcomes of our lives. But the Divine King of the universe has said in His Word that, "all the days ordained for me were written in your book before one of them came to be" (Psalm 139:16 NIV). He is God, and we are not. Satan doesn't want us to know that Truth and offers us a cheap imitation instead.

Feminism is another key component in Oprah's religion. Some have described her audience as a New Age feminist congregation.[13] The idea of victimhood plays well into the hands of women, in particular, who think that being born female instead of male is a burden that must be carried through life. Unfortunately, this radical idea not only surrounded the Church but has infiltrated it as well.

AN EXTREME MAKEOVER

Radical feminism has had a crippling effect on our culture for decades. Abortion on demand, no-fault divorce, and the rise in lesbianism have all served to help advance a deadly agenda based on the concept that women are victims. For years in Washington, I worked with organizations that would help to shepherd through Congress the passage of legislation to protect families, including both men *and* women. We did not see women as second-class citizens but viewed them as crucial to God's plan and purpose. Given the preponderance of extremely talented women with important and high profile jobs in Washington, it's hard to make the argument that women are victims. But, as is often said in the nation's capital, the idea of victimhood for women "plays well outside the Beltway."

Unfortunately, that idea also plays well in some churches too! Sophia is the New Age goddess of feminism, yet her history is as old as the most ancient civilizations. Both the Romans and the Greeks referred to this mythological goddess. The Greek word *sophia* means wisdom, and she is also referenced in the writings of the early Gnostics as well.

As the feminist theology continued to grow, as more liberal members of the clergy looked for ways to appease the feminist members of their congregations, Sophia worship expanded in popularity. But this pagan worship took center stage in 1993, when a conference entitled Re-Imagining took place in Minneapolis, Minnesota. The group holding the conference called themselves "mainline Protestant Christian feminists." The attendees openly chanted prayers to Sophia, declaring her the "divine energy" in women. One of the speakers, Delores Williams, a professor at Union Theological Seminary in New York, told the group, "I don't think we need a theory of atonement at all . . . atonement has to do so much with death . . . l don't think we need folks hanging on crosses, and blood dripping, and weird stuff . . . we just need to listen to the god within."[14] God was portrayed as an abusive parent, Jesus as an obedient child, and the Lord's death on the cross as the ultimate child abuse.

Each main speaker took the podium while the audience prayed, "Bless Sophia, dream the vision; share the wisdom dwelling deep within." Lesbianism among Christian women was extolled, declarations were made that Jesus was unnecessary because of Sophia, and a communion service was done with milk and honey, as utterances were made to "Our Maker, Sophia!"[15]

While it would be easier and perhaps more comforting to think this was some sort of singular, abhorrent conference in the early 1990s, that is not the case. More and more clergy are openly embracing this paganism, and some denominations now identify Sophia as the Holy Spirit in the Trinity. After all, they would argue, doesn't there have to be a *feminine* manifestation of God in His triune nature, or do we, as women, simply allow all these patriarchs to trample us under foot with their dominance? Yes, victimhood has now become more than just the stuff of bad TV afternoon talk shows. It is a deadly theology derived from the depths of hell.

The serpent slithers and hisses, asking over and over and over, "Did God *really* say?"

There are still false prophets and diviners in our midst, just as Jeremiah had warned the Babylonian captives so long ago. God knew that we could so easily be taken captive by bad ideas and He wanted His children then, just as He wants His children now, to know how to live abundantly as exiles. Deception is not a part of the prescription for successful living. Discernment is.

Many people today are walking around in spiritual darkness—people that "have neither knowledge nor understanding" (Psalm 82:5 ESV). They strut into Vanity Fair with no idea how threatening the marketplace can potentially be, not knowing how many charlatans and mountebanks occupy the public square. They merely happen upon the most popular booths, where millions of other "shoppers" have gathered to listen to a charismatic merchant hawk his or her goods. But too often they linger just long enough to "buy" and end up taking home counterfeit "goods."

While His children were in exile, God warned them, through the prophet Jeremiah, that false prophets and diviners would be "in their midst." They would practice deception by telling lies and making false statements. God also let His people know, in no uncertain terms, that "I did not send them!" (Jeremiah 29:9 ESV)

Charles Spurgeon once said that, "Discernment is not a matter of simply telling the difference between right and wrong; rather it is telling the difference between right and almost right."[16] The captives in Babylon would have to *learn to discern*—they would need to know the sharp distinction between the Truth and a lie. That same mandate and instruction applies to us today—a people *still* in captivity.

CONCLUSION
Victorious Living Behind Unseen Bars

Everyone has a spirit that can be refined, a body
that can be trained in some manner, a suitable path
to follow. You are here to realize your inner divinity
and manifest your innate enlightenment.

Morihei Ueshiba[1]

True believers are always represented as mixing in the
world, doing their duty in it, and glorifying God by
patience, meekness, purity, and courage in their several
positions—and not by cowardly desertion of them.
Moreover, it is foolish to suppose that we can keep the
world and the devil out of our hearts by going into holes
and corners! True religion and unworldliness are best
seen, not in timidly forsaking the post which God has
allotted to us—but in manfully standing our ground,
and showing the power of grace to overcome evil.

J. C. Ryle[2]

Fight the good fight of the faith. Take hold
of the eternal life to which you were called
and about which you made the good confession in the presence of many witnesses. I charge
you in the presence of God, who gives life to all things, and of
Christ Jesus, who in his testimony before Pontius Pilate made
the good confession, to keep the commandment unstained and
free from reproach until the appearing
of our Lord Jesus Christ.

Paul to Timothy, 1 Timothy 6:12–14 ESV

18
Free While Captive

Dear captives and exiles:

Build houses and live in them. Plant gardens and eat from them. Get married. Have children. Tell your children to have children. Seek the welfare of the city. And one more thing, watch out for those liars and deceivers in your midst.

Yours, in His name,

Jeremiah, the prophet

here, in summary, is the letter the Lord dictated to His weeping, lamenting prophet to be given to His people. Because of their disobedience, God's children found themselves living in a foreign land, with strange customs and pagan gods. They had been warned, and they knew their own tattered history of mixing belief in pagan gods with devotion to the One True God. The results were always disastrous. But they disobeyed nonetheless and became captives and exiles.

God, who never, *ever* stopped loving His children, wanted the people to live—abundantly! Through Jeremiah, God gave clear instructions for how that would be accomplished. Those instructions are just as applicable to us today, as we find ourselves captive in a hostile, pagan culture. God *still* wants us to live abundantly and boldly.

What we have done, through our journey into the marketplace of ideas, is discover how differently the world thinks from what the followers of the Word believe. At the center of all the "isms" and philosophies being bought and sold in Vanity Fair is Jesus. Either He *is* who He said He is, or He *is not*. If He is not, then everything written on the pages of this book (and far more importantly, of *His* book) matters very little and contains no truth. But, if Jesus is who He said He was, then we each must decide what to believe and how to live.

Neil Peart, the drummer for the band Rush, said, "Live for yourself—there's no one else more worth living for."[3] Compare Peart's statement to what the apostle Paul wrote to the church at Philippi while sitting in a prison cell in Rome: "For me, living means living for Christ, and dying is even better" (Phillippians 1:21 NLT). Which merchant are you listening to? What "message" will you buy?

PRACTICAL PACKING FOR THE PILGRIMAGE

Our pilgrimage *will* take us right into the center of Vanity Fair. There is simply no way around it. Go we must. How then can we effectively "influence and occupy" in the marketplace of ideas until the Lord either calls us home or until He returns? Are there ways to travel safely and triumphantly as we sojourn through this life? Without a doubt! As you prepare for the journey, here are some suggested travel items to carry in your backpack.

The ballot box

To begin with, "seeking the welfare of the city" can sometimes be difficult. It takes time and commitment. Let's start in a very profound yet practical way. Evidence abounds each time America enters into another election cycle. For some, this is a wearisome process; for others, it is the high privilege of casting their vote.

Hardly a day goes by in an election year that we, the people, are not afforded the opportunity to hear some candidate's position on a particular issue. Mass media has provided unprecedented platforms for individuals running for public office to advance their ideas, either through a series of televised debates or through paid political advertisements.

Every voting citizen is without excuse regarding knowing where a candidate stands and what his or her voting record has been. The Internet alone is a wellspring of information to assist us in making an informed choice before casting our ballot.

But for the follower of Jesus Christ, there is another layer that must be plumbed before we make our decision. First, the question must be asked, "Does God care if we vote?" The answer is a resounding *yes*! The Bible tells us to "seek the welfare of the city" (Jeremiah 29:7 ESV). Picking the right candidate puts the right people in place to advance the right public policy that shapes the right laws that protect the rights of the people! That results in the well-being of our nation and its citizens.

The next question is: "Does God care who we vote for?" Absolutely! Again, the Scriptures tell us that when "the godly are in authority, the people rejoice. But when the wicked are in power, they groan" (Proverbs 29:2 NLT). God's Word contains books like Judges and Kings, where we read the outcome of good leadership versus poor governance. Who we vote for can be, in the final outcome, the difference between rejoicing and groaning!

The final question is, "How do we decide who to vote for?" There is eloquence in the words of John Adams, America's second president and a Christian:

We electors have an important constitutional power placed in our hands; we have a check upon two branches of the legislature . . . the power I mean of electing at stated periods [each] branch. . . . It becomes necessary to every [citizen] then, to be in some degree a statesman, and to examine and judge for himself of the tendency of political principles and measures. Let us examine, then, with a sober, a manly . . . and a Christian spirit; let us neglect all party [loyalty] and advert to facts; let us believe no man to be infallible or impeccable in government any more than in religion; take no man's word against evidence, nor implicitly adopt the sentiments of others who may be deceived themselves, or may be interested in deceiving us.[4]

The mandate *to* and the solemnity *of* voting is clearly heard in Adams's remarks. He is challenging us to look inward *first* and know what we believe and why we believe it. Having a "Christian spirit" means having a mind that has been renewed through a relationship with Christ Himself. Our entire perspective on everything, including politics, is transformed completely when our hearts have been changed by the One who gave His life for us.

It was John Adams's second cousin, Samuel Adams, who is credited with significantly shaping the political culture of our new nation. Also a Christian, Samuel drew from his knowledge of Bible history to mold American history. In 1781, he wrote:

> Let each citizen remember at the moment he is offering his vote that he is not making a present or a compliment to please an individual—or at least that he ought not so to do; but that he is executing one of the most solemn trusts in human society for which he is accountable to God and his country.[5]

When we carefully and prayerfully prepare to cast our votes during an election—a marvelous way of obediently "influencing and occupying" until Jesus comes—it is imperative that each of us carry in our hearts the words of John and Samuel Adams as we enter the voting booth. May we never shrink back from the "seeking the welfare of the city" by exercising this most precious privilege of voting.

Willing hearts and helping hands

Biblical "city welfare seekers" serve where the needs are. They serve as volunteers at crisis pregnancy centers as a gentle yet exquisite way of countering the doctrine of death that pervades our culture. By manifesting the love of Christ at a rescue mission, they minister to those who have lost all hope and do it so much more effectively than any government program. They offer their time and talents to comfort those who live behind bars by sharing the hope of the Cross. No secular rehab program can do that and will never be as effective as the redemptive message of the Gospel news.

Christians run businesses built on biblical principles rather than on greedy thinking. They work as teachers and professors, molding the thinking of their students with a Christian worldview. They take up the calling of a public servant and serve God through government, or they offer their lives and their sacred honor by putting on the uniform of the United States military and serving where they are sent. Sometimes they use their platforms as professional athletes by showing the world, through the posture of prayer, to whom all glory and honor is to be given. Those who "seek the welfare of the city" know how to change the world around them, and they do! Prayerfully consider asking God where He would have *you* to serve. There is a hurting world all around us, dark corners of our culture where the Light of the World needs to go. Are you willing to carry His message, His truth, and His light into any and every part of our world? Consider the words of John Wesley: "One of the principal rules of religion is, to lose no occasion of serving God. And, since He is invisible to our eyes, we are to serve Him in our neighbour; which He receives as if done to Himself in person, standing visibly before us."[6]

The straight stick of truth

The Bible gives us a clear directive to "be diligent to present yourself approved to God, a worker who does not to be ashamed, rightly dividing the word of truth" (2 Timothy 2:15 NKJV). Who likes to do homework? Yet without it, how would we ever graduate to the next level? God directs that we should study His Word. It is to be written on the tablet of our hearts (Proverbs 7:3); we are to teach it to our children (Deuteronomy 11:19); and we are to allow it to light our path through life (Psalm 119:105).

In his second letter to Timothy, Paul instructs his student to study God's Word carefully and always to preach and teach it accurately and clearly. Paul then uses the phrase "rightly dividing" which, when translated, means "cutting it straight." This is perhaps why D. L. Moody so frequently referred to the Bible as God's "straight stick of Truth."[7] Just as a carpenter or a

***Let's be honest* with one another. It hurts to be called names, no matter how old you are.**

mason must be precise when practicing his trade, so must we be precise when we share the Word. It is *God's* Word, and it must always be handled with precision.

The only way we can gain that skill—that exactness—is by getting into the Scriptures on a regular basis. Quiet time set aside each day to hear what the Lord is saying to us, through His Word, is not only a necessity for knowing exactly who God is but it is the only way we can be protected from falling prey to the false prophets and diviners that are in our midst today! The "straight stick of truth" is the perfect meter for measuring all the crooked ideas that are being hawked in the marketplace today. Knowing Truth from falsehood presumes that we first know the Truth. There is no other way of determining what is untrue. John Chrysostom, an early Church father who lived during the mid-300s, made this point perfectly when he said, "To get the full flavor of an herb, it must be pressed between the fingers, so it is the same with the Scriptures; the more familiar they become, the more they reveal their hidden treasures and yield their indescribable riches."[8]

A heart like His

This just might be the most important item we place in our backpacks, and it is by far the most delicate. Let's be honest with one another. It hurts to be called names, no matter how old you are. I have received some pretty nasty emails in my life. and I do grow weary of being called a "kneejerk, reactionary homophobic, Bible-thumping member of the Religious Right." I've lost count of how many times I have been called that—in writing or on national television. But God has used all of those slings and arrows of outrageous criticism to break my heart, so that I might have a heart like His.

I once participated in a televised debate with the leading feminists of our time, including the president of the National Organization for Women. As I was being pilloried by the five (yes, *five*) feminists who had been booked to debate me (yes, *just* me), God did something remarkable. It felt as though, in the midst of the roar of the rowdy studio audience and the goading of the TV host, God was asking me to look at those five women the way He sees them. "Stop, and listen, *really* listen with the ears on your heart. Look beyond *what* they are saying, and hear *why* they are saying it."

Most, if not all, of the women had had abortions—some more than one. Nearly each one was divorced, was in a lesbian relationship, or both. They were angry, they were shrill, and they were *hurting*. God let me hear the pain that lay just below the rage. The insecurities they had about who they were and where they fit into the world stood in stark contrast to the peace, the unsurpassable peace that I had, knowing I was the daughter of the Most High King. They struggled with the idea of forgiveness from anyone, let alone from some supreme being, but I knew I had been forgiven and that my sins had been forgotten by the God who said He would remember them no more (Hebrews 8:12).

Because of what Jesus had done, the rage of these women could be replaced with forgiveness, their pain exchanged for peace, and their fear transformed to hope.

Suddenly I had to hold back the tears. I remembered in that moment a hill just outside of Jerusalem, not far from the city gates, where three crosses stood. On the middle cross, my Savior hung—*for me. My* sin, *my* guilt, *my* shame had put Him there. But He submitted to the will of His Father and poured out His life for *me*. He did it for those five feminists as well. He did not hang on the Cross any longer for their sins than He did for mine. And when He uttered the words that shook hell to its core—"*It is finished*"—the penalty, the wages of sin was paid, once and for all. The ransom was paid for my sins, for the sins of the five feminists in front of a national television audience, and for the sins of everyone watching the show—and beyond. The completed work of the Cross paid a debt that I owed. *Amazing grace!* How dare I be angry at these women? Because of what Jesus had done, the rage of these women could be replaced with forgiveness, their pain exchanged for peace, and their fear transformed to hope. Where they stood politically meant nothing compared to where these women stood spiritually. They needed to know that they could stand before the Cross and receive the gift of eternal life.

I'm not sure who won the debate that day, but I do know that I wrote their five names in my Bible and started to pray for them daily. I may never know whether they did make a decision to receive what Christ had done for them at Calvary—but I know I was called to love them and pray for them. Winning the debate wasn't the goal, winning them to Christ is.

A DANGEROUS JOURNEY AND A SAFE HOMECOMING

John Bunyan, a vain tinker turned preacher, knew the transforming power of the Cross. His life had been so radically changed after his conversion that, despite the political climate of his day, Bunyan simply could not stop telling anyone who would listen about the Good News. "Out of the abundance of the heart the mouth speaks" (Matthew 12:34 ESV). And—he *spoke*! It would cost Bunyan dearly as he would spend many long years in prison for the public proclamation of his faith. He knew far too well the result of promoting the Truth in a marketplace filled with lies. It was a dangerous journey for Bunyan, but he *could* not and *would* not stop. He pressed on—and so must we.

Out of the adversity of imprisonment, Bunyan wrote a classic that has been read by millions since it was written in 1676. Christians everywhere resonate with the picture Bunyan paints of what we, as believers, will encounter on our earthly journey. *Pilgrim's Progress* is replete with beautiful illustrations of how to apply biblical truth to the world around us. Do yourself a favor and read it from cover to cover. You needn't struggle with the versions written in an older and more difficult style. Modern language versions are readily available. In reading his work, you will be reminded again and again of the power, the authority, the consistency, and the Truth of God's Word.

Christian and Faithful entered, out of necessity, into Vanity Fair. We, too, shall find ourselves there. Like the two traveling companions, we will discover ourselves surrounded by stalls where every "foolish trifle" in the world is up for sale. The marketplace will be populated with cheats and rogues. Will we be tempted, like Christian and Faithful, to try to pass through unnoticed? Will we be threatened by the jeering from the crowds at the fair? Will we pull our "clothes" up around our faces, hoping the world won't notice we have entered into Vanity Fair? And when our presence *is* finally noted, and when the merchants start to shout out, "Buy, buy, *buy!*" how will we respond?

That's you and me.

We are the Truth lovers.

We cannot bypass this fair.

Despite the discomfort they felt and the fears they must have had, Christian and Faithful responded, *"We buy only the Truth!"* Their response reveals two very important things. First, they *knew* what the Truth was, and they could distinguish it from anything that wasn't the Truth. But their statement also intimates something else. Someone, somewhere in Vanity Fair had to have a booth where Truth was being offered. "Truth lovers" needed to "set up shop" in the marketplace, not only to offer comfort and sustenance to weary Pilgrims but to try and influence and deter the other merchants from selling their shabby goods.

That's you and me. We are the Truth lovers. We cannot bypass this fair. For, in the words of Bunyan, he that would bypass this town, "must needs go out of the world." Jesus called us to go "into the world." He never said it would be easy, but into this bustling fair we must go!

Charles Spurgeon, England's most prominent preacher for the last half of the nineteenth century, reminds us why going "into the world" is so crucial:

My brethren, let me say, be like Christ at all times. Imitate him in "public." Most of us live in some sort of public capacity—many of us are called to work before our fellow-men every day. We are

189

watched; our words are caught; our lives are examined—taken to pieces. The eagle-eyed, argus-eyed world observes everything we do, and sharp critics are upon us. Let us live the life of Christ in public. Let us take care that we exhibit our Master, and not ourselves—so that we can say, "It is no longer I that live, but Christ that lives in me."[9]

Fellow Pilgrim, I thank you for the privilege of walking with you a while on our journey. May I remind you, before we go our separate ways, of where our journey ends? Christian knew, Faithful knew, and Bunyan knew, and those of us who have received the gift of salvation know.

John Bunyan writes, at the end of *Pilgrim's Progress*, of the day Christian crossed through the misty River of Death and entered into the Celestial City. He tells how the Gates of Heaven opened and Christian looked, with amazement, at the streets paved with gold. After finally finishing his great journey, the Pilgrim passed through the mighty gates with a crown on his head because he had been made perfect through the work of the Cross. Bunyan writes that the bells of the City rang for joy, for Christian had come to his *true* home. Our true home—heaven!

The Israelites were captives in Babylon, John Bunyan was a captive in an English dungeon, and you and I are captives in a fallen world. Yet, in the midst of our captivity, we have been given instructions on how to live abundantly, obediently, and triumphantly. We have not been called "out of the world," but rather we are called to go directly into the center of Vanity Fair. It is part of our Pilgrim's progress.

For the sake of the Gospel, for the message of the Cross, for the love of our Savior, will you now enter into the marketplace of ideas?

Jesus prayed, "As you sent me into the world, so I have sent them into the world. And for their sake I consecrate myself, that they also may be sanctified in truth" (John 17:18–19 ESV). While our status may be that of captive, may we, like Christian and Faithful, carry His Truth into the world, with grace and boldness—so that many more shall someday proclaim, *"We only buy the Truth!"*

NOTES

Introduction: A Profane Pilgrim

1. John Bunyan, chapter two of *Grace Abounding to the Chief of Sinners*. www.www.worldinvisible.com/library/bunyan).

2. John Bunyan, "Reasons," in *The Struggler*. http://books.google.com.

3. Charles H. Spurgeon, quoted on the Bunyan Ministries website. www.bunyanministries.org.

4. John Owen, quoted in William P. Farley, "John Bunyan: The Faithful Tinker from Bedford," *Enrichment Journal*. http://enrichmentjournal.ag.org.

5. John Bunyan, "Prison Meditations: A Poem." Available at http://acacia.pair.com/Acacia.John.Bunyan/Poetry.

6. Linda K. Hughes and Michael Lund, *The Victorian Serial* (Charlottesville: University Press of Virginia, 1991), 5.

Chapter 1: The Marketplace

1. John Bunyan, the visit to Vanity Fair in *Pilgrim's Progress in Today's English* (Chicago: Moody Publishers, 1992), 89–90.

2. Ibid., 93.

3. Ibid., 97.

4. Daniel O. Teasley, "Light Breaks at Last."

Chapter 2: What, Me? An Exile?

1. George MacDonald, *Creation in Christ: Unspoken Sermons*, Rolland Hein, ed. (Vancouver B.C.: Regent College Publishing, 2004).

2. Henry Blackaby, "God's Invitation to Join Him in His Work," in *Experiencing God* (Nashville: B & H Publishing Group, 2009).

3. A. W. Tozer, quoted in James L. Snyder, *In Pursuit of God: The Life of A. W. Tozer* (Camp Hill, PA: Christian Publications, 1991).

Chapter 3: A Citizen of Two Worlds

1. St. Augustine, *The City of God*, Book XIV, chapter 1.

2. Ibid., Book XIX, Chapter 26.

3. Ibid.

4. Ibid.

5. Ibid.

6. Ibid., Book V, Chapter 24.

7. C. S. Lewis, *The Joyful Christian* (New York: Scribner, 1996), 138.

Chapter 4: Just Evangelize?

1. Warren Wiersbe, quoted in *Men of Integrity* magazine. www.christianitytoday.com.

2. Elias Boudinot, quoted in Bradley S. O'Learey, *God and America's Leaders: A Collection of Quotations by America's Presidents and Founding Fathers on God and Religion* (New York: WND Books, 2010).

3. William Booth, quoted in "William Booth: First General of the Salvation Army," *Christian History* magazine, issue 26. Posted online August 8, 2008. www.christianitytoday.com.

Chapter 5: A Living Letter to a Captive People

1. Ludwig von Mises, first lecture in *Economic Policy: Thoughts for Today and Tomorrow,* second edition, (The Ludwig von Mises Institute, 2002). http://mises.org.

2. Bureau of Labor Statistics, United States Department of Labor. Accessed March 2012 at http://data.bls.gov/timeseries.

3. David Zeiler, "Real Unemployment Rate Could Give Obama Heartburn in November," *Money Morning*, March 9, 2012. http://moneymorning.com/2012/03/09.

4. Terence P. Jeffrey, "Obama Added More to National Debt in First 19 Months than All Presidents from Washington through Reagan Combined, says Gov't Data," cnsnews.com, December 8, 2010. http://cnsnews.com/news/article.

5. Terence P. Jeffrey, "Obama Has Now Increased Debt More than All Presidents from Washington through George H.W. Bush Combined," cnsnews.com, October 5, 2011. http://cnsnews.com/news/article.

6. Federal Reserve Bank of Boston, "The Survey of Consumer Payment Choice," January 2010, quoted in Ben Woolsey and Matt Schulz, "Credit card statistics, industry facts, debt statistics," CreditCards.com updated Tuesday, March 27, 2012. www.creditcards.com.

7. Ben Woolsey and Matt Schulz, "Credit card statistics, industry facts, debt statistics," CreditCards.com updated Tuesday, March 27, 2012. www.creditcards.com.

8. The fictional character of Wilkins Micawber, in Charles Dickens's *David Copperfield*, published in 1849.

9. David Down, "Babylon the Golden," Digging Up the Past archive, 2010. Accessed March 2012 at www.diggingsonline.com.

10. Ibid.

11. Herodotus, Book 1, paragraph 178.

12. "The Ishtar Gate," Bible History Online. www.bible-history.com/archaeology/Babylon/ishtar-gate.html.

13. Down, "Babylon the Golden."

14. Martin Luther, "God's Unchanging Word," in John R. Rice's *742 Heartwarming Poems* (Murfreesboro, TN: Sword of the Lord Publishers, 1982), number 12.

Chapter 6: There's No Place Like Home

1. Winston Churchill, in an address to the House of Commons on November 16, 1948, regarding the birth of Prince Charles. http://hansard.millbanksystems.com.
2. Chuck Swindoll, quoted in Dennis Rainey, Charles R. Swindoll, and Roy Zuck, *Ministering to Twenty-First Century Families* (Nashville: Thomas Nelson, 2001).
3. Julie Schmit, "Home Prices Hit 2002 Levels," USA TODAY, June 3, 2011. www.usatoday.com/money/economy/housing.
4. See Pew Research Center, "Social networking sites and our lives," *Factbrowser*, June 16, 2011. www.factbrowser.com.
5. G. K. Chesterton, "Heretics," essay, 1905.

Chapter 7: Harvest from and for Heaven

1. Rudyard Kipling, "The Glory of the Garden," poem, 1911.
2. John Bunyan, *Pilgrim's*, 108.
3. Barna Group, "New Study Shows Trends in Tithing and Donating," April 14, 2008. www.barna.org/barna-update/.

Chapter 8: I Do, I Did, I Will

1. Jeremy Taylor, from a sermon called "The Marriage Ring," in *The Whole Works of the Right Rev. Jeremy Taylor, D.D.*, vol. 4 (London: Longman, Green, Longman, & Roberts, 1862).
2. William Tyndale, "Obedience of a Christian Man," in *Doctrinal treatises and introductions to different portions of the Holy Scriptures* (Cambridge: University Press, 1848).
3. William Barclay, *The Letters to the Corinthians* (Louisville, KY: Westminster John Knox Press), 117.

Chapter 9: What God Has Joined Together

1. Pew Research Center, "The Decline of Marriage and Rise of New Families," November 18, 2010. http://pewsocialtrends.org.
2. Ibid.
3. Ibid.
4. Ibid.
5. Ibid.
6. Centers for Disease Control, "CDC Connection: For the Advisory Committee to the Director—December 2011." www.cdc.gov.
7. Guttmacher Institute, "U.S. Teenage Pregnancies, Births and Abortions: National

and State Trends and Trends by Race and Ethnicity," January 2010 (Guttmacher Institute). www.guttmacher.org.

8. Dan Quayle, speech at the Commonwealth Club in San Francisco, May 19, 1992.

9. "Dan Quayle vs. Murphy Brown," *Time* magazine, June 1, 1992. www.time.com/time/magazine.

10. Barbara Dafoe Whitehead, "Dan Quayle Was Right," *The Atlantic*, April 1993. www.theatlantic.com/magazine/archive.

11. Ibid.

12. U.S. Census Bureau, "Number, Timing and Duration of Marriages and Divorces: 2009," issued May, 2011. www.census.gov.

13. Ibid.

14. Ibid.

15. Ibid.

16. Attributed to Groucho Marx, comedian.

17. U.S. Census Bureau, "Number, Timing."

18. Pew Research Center, "The Decline of Marriage and Rise of New Families," November 18, 2010. http://pewsocialtrends.org.

19. U.S. Census Bureau, "Number, Timing."

20. Mary Kay Blakely, *American Mom* (New York: Simon & Schuster, 1995).

21. C. S. Lewis, *Letters of C. S. Lewis* (Orlando, FL: Mariner Books, 2003), 429.

22. Pew Research Center, "The Decline of Marriage."

23. Belinda Luscombe, "Who Needs Marriage? A Changing Institution," *Time* magazine, Thursday, November 16, 2010. www.time.com/time/magazine.

24. Ibid.

25. "Couples Who Cohabit Before Engagement Are More Likely to Struggle," *ScienceDaily*, July 13, 2009. www.sciencedaily.com

26. Jean Kerr, *Mary, Mary* (New York: Dramatists Play Service, Inc. 1965), 19.

27. Robert Andersen, *Double Solitaire* (New York: Dramatists Play Service, Inc. 1972).

Chapter 10: The Cenote of Sacrifice

1. Margaret Sanger, *Women and the New Race* (New York: Eugenics Publishing Co., 1920, 1923).

2. Tertullian, *Apologia*, 9.

3. Steven Ertelt, "United States Sees 53 Million Abortions Since Roe in 1973," Lifenews.com, 11/26/10. www.lifenews.com.

4. R. K. Jones and M. L. Kavanaugh, "Changes in abortion rates between 2000 and 2008 and lifetime incidence of abortion, *Obstetrics & Gynecology*, 2011, 117(6):1358–1366.

5. R. K. Jones, L. B. Finer, and S. Singh, *Characteristics of U.S. Abortion Patients 2008* (New York: Guttmacher Institute, 2010).

6. Ibid.

7. R. K. Jones, et al., "Repeat Abortion in the United States," *Occasional Report, no 29* (New York: Guttmacher Institute, 2006).

8. Jones, *Characteristics*.

9. "U.S.A.: People QuickFacts," U.S. Census 2010. http://quickfacts.census.gov.

10. Jones, *Characteristics*.

11. The Center for Bio-Ethical Reform, "Abortion Facts," www.abortionno.org/resources/fastfacts.

12. S. K. Henshaw, "Unintended Pregnancy in the United States," *Family Planning Perspectives*, 1998, 30(1):24–29, 46; and R. K. Jones and M. L. Kavanaugh, "Changes in abortion rates between 2000 and 2008 and lifetime incidence of abortion, *Obstetrics & Gynecology*, 2011, 117(6).

13. Randall K. O'Bannon, PhD., "Abortion Giant Planned Parenthood: Now Nearly a Billion Dollar Corporation," *National Right to Life News*, vol. 34 (7) 2007, 8. www.nrlc.org.

14. Ibid.

15. David Shaw, Times staff writer, "Abortion Bias Seeps into the News," *Los Angeles Times*, July 1, 1990. www.groupscsail.mit.edu.

16. Sarah Kliff, "'Pro-Life' or 'Anti-Abortion Rights'? Journalists, Abortion, and Why Word Choice Matters," *Newsweek*, March 19, 2010. www.thedailybeast.com.

17. Ann Oldenburg, "'Grey's Anatomy' abortion reaction? 'Quiet,'" *USA Today*, September 29, 2011. http://content.usatoday.com.

18. Maya, "I'm rooting for an abortion this Friday night," Feministing blog, July 9, 2010. http://community.feministing.com.

19. Joe Piazza, "Abortion No Longer Taboo Topic on Prime Time Television," Fox News, November 2, 2011. FoxNews.com.

20. Ibid.

21. Gerald Dickler, *On Trial: History-Making Trials from Socrates to Oppenheimer* (New York: Gramercy Books, 1962), 350–51.

22. John Bunyan, *Pilgrim's Progress*, 138–39.

23. Richard D. Younger, "Southern Grand Juries and Slavery," *The Journal of Negro History*, vol. 40 (2), April 1955, 166.

24. The Friends of Liberty and Equality, *An Address to the People of North Carolina on the Evils of Slavery*, electronic edition (Manumission Society of North Carolina, 2001), 6, proposition 1.V.

25. Philip A. Bolling, quoted in Daniel Reaves Goodloe, *The Southern Platform* (Boston: J. P. Jewett and Co., 1858), 49. http://books.google.com.

26. Carl N. Degler, *The Other South: Southern Dissenters in the Nineteenth Century* (New York: Harper & Row, 1974) 34.

27. Care Net, 2012, www.care-net.org., and Pro-Life Action League, Q&A:Abortion, 2012, http://prolifeaction.org.

28. Dr. Seuss, quoted in Edward Weseman, *Looking Tall by Standing Next to Short People* (Bloomington, IN: Authorhouse, 2007), 71.

29. Dr. Seuss, *Horton Hears a Who* (New York: Random House Books for Young Readers, 1954), 47.

30. Winston Churchill, speech in the House of Commons, May 17, 1916.

Chapter 11: Nothing New under the Sun

1. Peggy Noonan, American speechwriter, journalist, author.

2. Joycelyn Elders, Surgeon General of the United States 1993–94, in a speech in Austin, Texas, January 21, 1994.

3. James Russell Lowell, "The Present Crisis," stanza 8. www.readbookonline.net.

Chapter 12: A Perverse Twist of the Truth

1. Simone de Beauvoir, French writer and feminist (1908–1986), quoted in David Knox and Caroline Schact, *Choices in Relationships* (Independence, KY: Cengage Learning, 2009), 251.

2. Charles Colson, from radio broadcast "BreakPoint," July 12, 2011. (Prison Fellowship Ministries, 2011).

3. "Action Statement Preamble to the Platform," Platform of the 1993 March on Washington for Lesbian, Gay, and Bi Equal Rights and Liberation, Queer Resource Directory, www.qrd.org.

4. John Shelby Spong, *The Sins of Scripture* (New York: HarperCollins, 2005).

5. C. S. Lewis, *Mere Christianity* (New York: Macmillan, 1960), 96.

6. Jeremy Taylor, from a sermon called "The Marriage Ring," in *The Whole Works of the Right Rev. Jeremy Taylor, D.D.*, vol. 4 (London: Longman, Green, Longman, & Roberts, 1862).

Chapter 13: A Marriage Made in Heaven

1. Andrea Dworkin, quoted in D. Kelly Weisberg, *Applications of Feminist Legal Theory to Women's Lives* (Philadelphia: Temple University Press, 1996), 149.

2. Thornton Wilder, words spoken by a character in the play *Skin of Our Teeth*, Act II.

3. The Heritage Foundation, "The Benefits of Marriage," 2012, www.familyfacts.org/briefs.

4. John Adams, in a letter to Thomas Jefferson, July 16, 1814.

5. Thomas DeWitt Talmage, American clergyman, 1823–1903.

6. CBN News, "UK Upholds Fine Against Christian Hotel Owners," Monday, February 20, 2012. www.cbn.com.

7. Christina Ng, "Texas Macy's Employee Fired for Allegedly Violating Store's LGBT Policy," ABC News, December 8, 2011. http://abcnews.co.com.

8. "Christian Foster Couple Lose 'Homosexuality Views' Case," BBC News, February 28, 2011. www.bbc.co.uk.
9. "Christian Preacher Vows to Fight after He's Arrested for 'Public Order' Offences after Saying Homosexuality Is a Sin," Mail Online, April 4, 2012, UK Daily Mail, www.dailymail.co.uk.
10. "Atty Says School Threatened, Punished Boy Who Opposed Gay Adoption," Radio Fox News, January 24, 2012. http://radio.foxnews.com.
11. Bunyan, *Pilgrim's*, 99–102.
12. Ibid., 101–102.
13. "Stand Up, Stand Up for Jesus," hymn text by George Duffield, Jr. 1818–1888 and music by George J. Webb, 1803–1887. www.hymnsite.com.
14. Bunyan, *Pilgrim's*, 103.

Chapter 14: Winsome Words of Welfare Seekers

1. Christopher Hitchens, quoted in "Editorial: What Hitchens and Tebow Shared," *USA Today*, December 19, 2011. www.usatoday.com.
2. Samuel Adams, founding father, in the *Boston Gazette*, 1781. http://founders-quotes.com.
3. William Blake, *The Life of William Blake*, vol. II, (1863).

Chapter 15: City Builders, Past and Present

1. Joseph Goebbels, German minister of propaganda, 1933–1945, *Dissent and Truth*.
2. William O. Douglas, in *The Douglas Letters: Selections from the Private Papers of Justice William O. Douglas* (1987). 1976 Letter to Young Lawyers Section of the Washington State Bar Association.
3. "Abolitionists," www.us-civilwar.com.
4. James M. McPherson, *The Abolitionist Legacy: From Reconstruction to the NAACP*, (Princeton, NJ: Princeton University Press , 1995) 152.
5. Richard D. Younger, "Southern Grand Juries and Slavery," *The Journal of Negro History*, vol. 40 (2), April 1955, 166.
6. The Friends of Liberty and Equality, *An Address to the People of North Carolina on the Evils of Slavery*, electronic edition (Manumission Society of North Carolina, 2001), 6, proposition 1.V.
7. Philip A. Bolling, quoted in Daniel Reaves Goodloe, *The Southern Platform* (Boston: J. P. Jewett and Co., 1858), 49. http:/books.google.com.
8. Salvation Army, "History," www.salvationarmydfw.org.
9. Vachel Lindsay, "General William Booth Enters into Heaven," in Jessie B. Rittenhouse, ed., *The Second Book of Modern Verse* (Boston: Houghton Mifflin, 1920).
10. Ibid.
11. Arthur Tappan Pierson, *George Müller of Bristol* (London: James Nisbet & Co., 1899), 301.

12. William Booth, *The General's Letters 1885* (London: Salvation Army, 1990), 4.

Chapter 16: Wicked Wolves with Wily Words
1. Bishop John Shelby Spong, *Rescuing the Bible from Fundamentalism* (New York: HarperCollins, 1992) 5.
2. Francis Schaeffer, *Letters of Francis A. Schaeffer* (Wheaton, IL: Crossway Books, 1986), 80.
3. Bruce Bawer, *Stealing Jesus: How Fundamentalism Betrays Christianity* (New York: Three Rivers Press, 1997), 6–7.
4. Ibid.
5. Ibid.
6. A. W. Tozer, *Of God and Men* (Camp Hill, PA: Christian Publications, 1995).
7. Robert Funk, *The Acts of Jesus* (San Francisco: HarperSanFrancisco, 1998).
8. http://johnshelbyspong.com.
9. John Shelby Spong, *A New Christianity for a New World* (New York: HarperCollins, 2001), 2.
10. Ibid.
11. Ibid., 3.
12. Ibid., 2.
13. Watchman Nee, quoted in Ron Durham, *Ancient Words* (Maitland, FL: Xulon Press, 2011), 151.
14. Rob Bell, *Love Wins: A Book about Heaven, Hell and the Fate of Every Person who Ever Lived* (Grand Rapids: Zondervan, 2011).
15. Ibid.

Chapter 17: Psychic Friends?
1. Derek Acorah, quoted in The Psychics website, "Ghost Hunting with Derek Acorah," 2011, accessed April 5, 2012. www.the-psychics.co.uk.
2. C. S. Lewis, *Mere Christianity* (New York: Macmillian, 1960), book 2, chapter 1.
3. www.deepakchopra.com.
4. Deepak Chopra, *The Third Jesus* (New York: Three Rivers Press, 2008), 162–164.
5. Ibid., 71.
6. Ibid., 36, 62, 67, 70, 176, et al.
7. Neale Donald Walsch, *Conversations with God: Book 1* (New York: G.P. Putnam's Sons, 1996).
8. Jessie McKinley, "The Wisdom of the Ages, for Now Anyway," *New York Times*, March 23, 2008. www.nytimes.com.
9. Ken MacQueen, "Eckhart Tolle vs. God," October 22, 2009, Macleans.ca, www2.macleans.ca.

10. Eckhart Tolle, *A New Earth* (New York: Penguin, reprint ed., 2008), 71.

11. Eva Illouz, *Oprah Winfrey and the Glamour of Misery* (New York: Columbia University Press, 2003).

12. "God whispers to us in our pleasures, speaks in our conscience, but shouts in our pains: it is His megaphone to rouse a deaf world." C. S. Lewis, *The Problem of Pain*.

13. Mark Oppenheimer, "The Church of Oprah Winfrey and the Theology of Suffering," *New York Times*, May 27, 2011. www.nytimes.com.

14. Delores Williams, "Re-Imagining Jesus," 1993 Re-Imagining Conference audiotapes (Apple Valley, MN: Resource Express), album 1, tape 3-2.

15. Kathy Kersten, "A New Heaven and a New Earth," *First Things*, March 1994. www.firstthings.com.

16. Charles Spurgeon, quoted in Tim Challies, *Discipline of Spiritual Discernment* (Wheaton, IL: Crossway Books, 2007), 1.

Chapter 18: Free While Captive

1. Morihei Ueshiba and John Stevens, *The Art of Peace* (Boston: Shambala Publications, 2010), 3.

2. J. C. Ryle, *Practical Religion* (Carlisle, PA: Banner of Truth, 1998), 293.

3. Neil Peart, Canadian songwriter, "Anthem," 1975.

4. John Adams, *Papers of John Adams* (Cambridge, MA: Harvard University Press, 1977), 81.

5. Samuel Adams, from *The Boston Gazette*, April 16, 1781, in *The Writings of Samuel Adams*, Harry Alonzo Cushing, editor (New York: G. P. Putnam's Sons, 1907), vol. IV, 256.

6. John Wesley, *Sermons on Several Occasions* (London: J. Grabham and W. Pine, 1760), 288.

7. D. L. Moody, quoted in William Backus, *Telling Each Other the Truth* (Bloomington, MN: Bethany House, 2006), 31.

8. John Chrysostom, quoted in Ronald Hennies and Sonia Weiss, *The Everything Prayer Book* (Avon, MA: Adams Media, 2003), 215.

9. Charles Spurgeon, "Christ's People—Imitators of Him," *Sermons of Rev. C. H. Spurgeon of London* (New York: R. Carter and Bros., 1883) 263.

TUNE IN TO HEAR JANET ON
MOODY RADIO

MOODYRADIO
Where you turn. For life.

In the Market with Janet Parshall challenges listeners to examine major news stories and issues being debated in the marketplace of ideas and speaks to them with the Word of God. In this fast-paced, caller-driven program, Janet evaluates newsworthy topics with guests and listeners using the Bible as a framework for discussion. This daily program addresses relevant issues important to Christians, with an engaging mix of listener interaction and commentary from highly respected guests.

www.InTheMarketWithJanetParshall.org

MOODYRADIO

Where you turn. For life.